Christian Homeschooling

Foundation & Practice

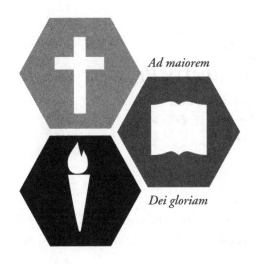

Ad maiorem

Dei gloriam

Christian Liberty Press

General editorship by Mark Beuligmann
Layout and editing by Edward J. Shewan
Copyediting by Diane Olson
Cover design by Bob Fine

A publication of
Christian Liberty Press
502 West Euclid Avenue
Arlington Heights, IL 60004
www.homeschools.org

Scripture references are conformed to The Holy Bible, New King James Version ©1982, Thomas Nelson, Inc.

ISBN 1-930367-76-7

Set in Berkeley
Printed in the United States of America

Table of Contents

Introduction

The Value of Christian Schools[1]

The Christian schools ought indeed to be welcomed even from the point of view of a merely secular broadening of the mind. They ought to be welcomed by every friend of real education simply because they tend to liberate our people from the dead hand of monopolistic state control which keeps education in a miserable rut and checks true intellectual advance. Even in their mere capacity as private schools they are worthy of all support.

But incomparably greater is their value as *Christian* schools. As Christian schools, they are like a precious salt amid our people, a precious salt that checks the ravages of decay; as Christian schools, too, they offer blessings with which all the blessings of this world are not worthy to be compared; they offer a liberty of which that lost civil liberty … is but a by-product; they offer the liberty with which Christ has made us free.

One word more needs to be spoken. What has Christianity to do with education: What is there about Christianity which makes it necessary that there should be Christian schools?

Very little, some people say. Christianity, they say, is a life, a temper of soul, not a doctrine or a system of truth; it can provide its sweet aroma, therefore, for any system which secular education may provide; its function is merely to evaluate whatever may be presented to it by the school of thought dominant at any particular time.

This view of the Christian religion … is radically false. Christianity is, indeed, a way of life; but it is a way of life founded upon a system of truth. That system of truth is of the most comprehensive kind; it clashes with opposing systems at a thousand points. The Christian life cannot be lived on the basis of anti-Christian thought. Hence the necessity of the Christian school.

---

1. This selection is taken from J. Gresham Machen's *The Christian School: The Out-Flowering of Faith* (Grand Rapids, MI: National Union of Christian Schools, 1934).

In a book written by two radically skeptical writers, John Herman Randall and John Herman Randall, Jr., there is an interesting passage. "Evangelical orthodoxy," say these skeptical writers, "thrives on ignorance and is undermined by education; Catholic orthodoxy is based on conviction, and has an imposing educational system of its own."[2] Is that dictum of these brilliant skeptical writers true? I am bound to say that it may seem to have a certain sting of truth about it. When we contemplate a type of Protestant orthodoxy that is content to take forlorn little shreds of Christian truth and tag them here and there upon a fundamentally anti-Christian or non-Christian education, and when we contrast such a procedure with the great system of Roman Catholic schools and the serious, comprehensive effort which the Roman Catholic Church makes to inform and mould human life, we can well understand the contrast so humiliating to Protestantism, which the Randalls have so forcibly drawn. Yet the dictum is not true; and in proof of the fact that it is not true I point ... to your Christian schools. You at least are seeking to oppose a Christian system to the system of this world; you at least are not making the huge mistake of trying to found the gold and silver and brass and iron of Christian theological seminaries or Christian colleges upon the clay feet of non-Christian schools; you at least are not appealing to ignorance, but you believe that real Christianity should have an educational system of its own. God grant that other Christian people may follow your example! You are the torchbearers of real advance for the whole Protestant Church. You have pointed out the way. God grant to others the grace to follow you! Thus and thus only will the darkness of ignorance be dispelled and the light of Christian truth be spread abroad in the land.

J. Gresham Machen

---

2.   John Herman Randall and John Herman Randall, Jr., *Religion and the Modern World*, 1929, p. 136.

PART 1

The Foundation of Christian Homeschooling

What is Christian Education?

by Eric D. Bristley

As Dr. D. James Kennedy avows, "Few Americans realize that, from 1620 when the Pilgrims landed until 1837, virtually all education in this country was private and Christian."[3] In the light of this great heritage, we as parents should seek to recapture the vision of our God-given responsibility of bringing up our children "in the training and admonition of the Lord" (Ephesians 6:4). In so doing, we must embrace a biblical philosophy of education, provide a biblical curriculum that reflects the Christian worldview in each subject, and practice a biblical method of teaching that seeks to make disciples of Christ. Our ultimate goal as Christian home educators is to glorify God and enjoy Him forever.

Biblical Foundation

Christian home educators should be committed to an educational philosophy which is not after the traditions of men, or the principles of this world, but after Christ, "in whom are hidden all the treasures of wisdom and knowledge" (Colossians 2:3). *Christian education means that Christ is central to education.* Consequently, our educational theory, methods, and practice must be built upon Christ as their cornerstone. But how can we know Christ apart from His Word which is the truth? The sacred Scriptures are the Word of Christ written. In them God has revealed Himself and His saving purpose in Christ.

Because there is only one God and one Christ, there is only one truth. This truth is the center and criterion of Christian education.

---

3. From the Foreword by Dr. D. James Kennedy to Christopher J. Klicka's *The Right Choice: The Incredible Failure of Public Education and the Rising Hope of Home Schooling* (Sisters, OR: Loyal Publishing, 1995), p. 6.

While the Bible is not used as the textbook in every subject, it is the foundational handbook for every course and the standard for teaching. As the foundational book, Scripture is the only infallible rule for faith and practice, for grammar and literature, for mathematics and science, for health and physical education, for geography and history, and for social studies and the arts. The beginning of wisdom is the fear of God.

Biblical Principles

For education to be consistently Christian it must self-consciously teach all subjects in the framework of biblical authority. To accomplish this we must have a methodology that guarantees its biblical character; the proper methodology, therefore, is to use the Bible in each and every course both directly and indirectly. It is applied *directly* when we derive our understanding of each topic from the actual statements of the Bible and using the text of Scripture appropriately in each subject. It is applied *indirectly* as we work out the implications of biblical truth as the proper framework for understanding each subject.

These basic principles and fundamental truths are the teachings of Scripture. *Biblical doctrines must regulate the way we teach and learn.* One key goal of Christian education is to teach students to reason biblically. Because of this, the educational process must show how the doctrinal truths of God's Word provide students with the Christian worldview. This worldview is a unified system of principles that guides the way we educate. It requires that every thought be made captive to the obedience of Jesus Christ (2 Corinthians 10:5).

Christian home educators, who are committed to the Bible as the standard for education, should seek to interpret God's Word in line with the *authority* of biblical truth and the *faith* of historic Christianity. This authority and faith is outlined by the following biblical principles:

The Sovereign Triune God

The most fundamental teaching of the Bible is the sovereignty of the Triune God. This truth is foundational for all Christian teaching. It alone separates Christian education from all forms of humanism and naturalism. Education which is truly and distinctly Christian must be dedicated to the glory of God above all else. Because the Creator is the sovereign God, He is Lord of Heaven and Earth, and He speaks with absolute authority about all things. There is nothing in this universe which can be truly learned apart from Him. He speaks as the Triune God. Unity in education is possible only on the basis of one God who is absolutely self-existent and independent of His creation. As the Trinity, He is the source of both unity and diversity in the world and in human life, for He exists as one God in three Persons.

Creation in Six Days

When God created all things in the universe *ex nihilo* (out of nothing) in six days, He created everything with meaning and purpose. Since all studies deal in one way or another with God's creation, all studies should be subordinate to God's revelation concerning His handiwork. The way to properly understand any subject is to study it in relation to its Creator. Because God created all things, there is nothing unknown to Him. Consequently, God's understanding—not man's—is first. All facts take their significance from the place God has assigned to them in creation. There are no uninterpreted facts which man can ever discover. Without God's revealed truth, these facts cannot be properly selected, systematized, and given a meaningful interpretation. Without the framework of a biblical worldview all education in science is futile.

Man, the Image of God

Because God created man in His own image, the ultimate purpose, meaning, and standards for human life and society come from God. Christian education must therefore reject all speculations of the evolutionary theory of human origins and rights. Man is a unique creature of God formed distinct from the animals. Endowed by his Creator with the gifts of religion, language, reason, choice, creativity, and society, man is like God in every way a creature can be. Created to serve and glorify God in the earth, Adam and Eve in the Garden of Eden talked directly with God and received from Him their original education. God taught man the truth about his role in the universe and his relationships with other people. God taught them that their most fundamental relationship is with Him as their Creator. Culture, society, and education are thus bound to religion. The student must be continually confronted with this pivotal truth about himself and society.

Man's Fall into Sin

The biblical record of the fall of Adam has serious and far-reaching implications for all of education. Because of the fall, man's entire nature as well as all of human society has been corrupted by sin. Not only is his heart hostile to God and His law, but his will is enslaved to corruption, and his mind is darkened by error. His whole nature has been corrupted by the evil influence of sin. Because of this, Christian education cannot start in a supposedly neutral fashion as though the child were an innocent person who simply needs the spark of goodness to be ignited within him.

Likewise, the human teacher is also corrupted by sin and does not always properly present God's truth. Because of sin's power, the teacher must acknowledge that he cannot change the heart of the student. Because sin has corrupted the whole of human thought and education throughout history, unbelieving scholarship can have a pervasive influence even upon those who seek to teach from a biblical worldview. The Christian teacher must grow in awareness of the influence of the sin that affects his thinking from his educational background and the society around him. Apart from abiding in Christ and His truth, he is liable to be made captive to ideas promoted by the various forms of the non-Christian worldview.

Christ the Redeemer

As a result of Adam's sin, God and man have become alienated. But God, in His grace, took the initiative to restore the relationship. After setting forth the requirements of redemption in the Old Testament, He fulfilled them in the New Testament in His Son, Jesus Christ. The Messiah came as the second Adam to undo the sin of the first Adam and its results. As the perfect Son of God, He became man and was crucified as the only Redeemer of mankind. By His redemptive work, Christ restores believers to a right relationship with their Creator. This restoration involves education. As part of His mediatorial work, Christ has an educational program which involves teaching all the things He has commanded. Christ teaches His people as the Bible is read, taught, and applied. All Christian education must therefore be subject to Christ as God's final Prophet, Priest, and King.

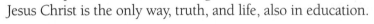

Jesus Christ is the only way, truth, and life, also in education.

The Holy Spirit and Salvation

Jesus Christ sent the Holy Spirit to teach the truth. The Holy Spirit is the only One who can make Christian education effective. For the teacher, to impart wisdom is a gift of God. For the student's heart to be opened to God's truth, a change of heart is required. In the new birth, the Spirit opens the mind and frees the will to embrace Christ by faith. Without this new birth, the Bible will never be the ultimate authority over the student's reasoning. Faith is the proper response to biblical truth, the only means by which the heart submits to it. While Christian education can be used by the Holy Spirit to bring the student to saving faith and to benefit a student after he comes to faith, ideally its full effect comes to those who already believe. Without faith, Christian education is ineffectual. Thus, both the teacher and the student are dependent upon the Holy Spirit and His work of grace.

The Holy Spirit uses believers as a means of leading students to Christ, in Whom are hidden all the treasures of wisdom and knowledge. Christian parents have the unique opportunity and privilege to train up their children in the fear and admonition of Christ. By combining teaching with prayer, exhortation, and discipline, the parent can be used by God to disciple his children to Christ. Thus Christian education, while not to be reduced to evangelism, will include the positive presentation of gospel truth as the answer to the ultimate questions in each subject. The gospel will be proclaimed as the answer to the student's deepest need for purpose, meaning, and goals in learning.

The Kingdom of Christ and the Antithesis

Because the Word of God is the only standard for education, Christian education is at odds with all pagan thought. Since it is part of Christ's program for building His kingdom, Christian education is engaged in spiritual and intellectual warfare with the kingdom of darkness. The fact of the new birth creates a distinction between two types of people—Christians and non-Christians. Christians are bringing every thought captive to the obedience of Christ and earnestly contending for the faith. The non-Christian, however, looks to man as the standard of all things, reasons according to the flesh, and calls his education neutral.

Because all education is inescapably religious, it can never take place in an ideological vacuum. Neutrality is impossible; for the educational worldview will either be Christian or non-Christian. Christ clearly taught, "He who is not with Me is against Me, and he who does not gather with Me scatters abroad" (Matthew 12:30). Therefore all non-Christian education is ultimately anti-Christian because it does not submit to the claims of Jesus Christ. Well-trained Christian students must be prepared to battle intellectually against the spirit of this age with an aggressive yet humble approach; therefore, Christian home educators seek to help train Christian warriors and leaders who will go forth in the power of the Holy Spirit to win decisive victories for the honor, glory, and kingdom of Christ.

The Return of Christ

Christian education is a part of God's purpose to put everything in creation under the feet of Christ. Christ is now reigning, but not everyone has bowed the knee to His authority. Not every area of life and thought has been made subject to Him. Christian education serves as part of His purpose to subdue people from all nations to the glory of God. He is calling out a people unto Himself who will learn His ways. Christian education is never an end in itself, but serves to magnify the glory of God. It should never lose sight of the fact that there is no final perfection in human life, society, or in education itself apart from the appearance of Jesus Christ. At His return, Christ will bring a conclusion to history through judgment of both the living and the dead.

Biblical Worldview Curriculum

The fear of the Lord is the beginning of wisdom, not only in our educational philosophy, but also for each discipline of study. Education is not made Christian by merely adding a course in Bible, or by beginning a class in prayer. If the course content or teaching method is humanistic, Christian supplements will do little to change the orientation. A Christian curriculum must derive its fundamental principles from God's Holy Word and work these out in a self-conscious manner. Christian home educators should seek to provide students with these principles as well as the content and skills which enable them to develop a biblical worldview in each subject. The following is an overview of such a curriculum.

Biblical Studies

Foundational to the Christian curriculum is the study of the Bible. Students need to be mastered by the Word of God before they can properly evaluate the writings of men. Bible study focuses the student's attention on the inspired text of the Bible as they are taught to understand and interpret it correctly. Its purpose is not the mere study of religion, nor even historical studies of Bible characters, but to arrive at a unified understanding of the biblical system of truth. It is this system of truth that provides the fundamental principles of a Christian worldview which must be applied to every area of life and thought.

To properly learn each subject, the student must not only be able to read, but he must also have the standard by which to judge what he reads. Therefore, the very first book a child should be taught is the Holy Bible. The Bible is the mind of God revealed to man. From it we learn about the creation, the fall into sin, and God's gracious plan of redemption. It is this knowledge which provides the key to correct understanding and enables the student to correctly interpret all he learns in the light of God's truth.

A Biblical View of Language and Literature

In the beginning God spoke and it came to pass. The three Persons of the Trinity have spoken to each other eternally. When God created man in His own image, He gave him the gift of language. The Bible tells us that after the Great Flood, the whole earth used the same language. Men, however, sought unity apart from God when they built the Tower of Babel. Seeing this, God confused their one language by changing it into many languages, and scattered them abroad over the face of the whole earth. Language thus originated with God, and is to be used for His glory. Men in their sin misuse and corrupt this gift. To discern the proper use of language, we need to study the Bible. It is only from the Bible that we come to know truth and error.

Reading and writing are foundational skills each child must learn. Without reading, they cannot study the Bible for themselves. Reading and writing are also basic to learning all other subjects in the light of God's Word. The teaching of phonics, therefore, is very important. If students cannot read the Bible, they will be truly illiterate. They must be taught to read, write, speak, study, and think in terms of the Word that makes language and life meaningful. They must develop the linguistic abilities that God has given them to glorify Himself. Language skills thus are not neutral, but must be oriented toward reading, writing, and speaking the truth in love.

Because language is thought expressed, and thoughts are never neutral, all literature has a religious point of view. Therefore, when reading *any* kind of literature, the question should be asked: Is the author Christian or non-Christian? If non-Christian, from what religious point of view is he writing? Most importantly, how does the author's message compare with what the Bible teaches? Students must learn to read and evaluate all human literature from the perspective of Scripture truth.

While it is important to acquaint students with the great literature which has helped shape Western Civilization, the study of such great books must be subject to the greatest book—the Bible. After learning the Bible properly, the student will be equipped to judge the words of human authors by the Word of truth. The student should learn to prize not only great classics, but distinguish Christian classics from the classics of unbelief. The great classics of the Christian heritage will inspire and challenge both teacher and student to follow Christ more completely.

The Biblical View of Mathematics

As Trinity, God is the reason why there is both unity and diversity in creation. This is the basis for unity and differentiation in mathematics. The Bible teaches us that the Creator is a God of order (1 Corinthians 14:33). As we study the created universe we are impressed with its mathematical order. Creation is governed by mathematical laws which reflect the character of the One who made it. Many of the laws of creation are described in terms of mathematics. When presented with the marvelous precision in nature and physics, the student should be led to marvel at God's mathematical ingenuity. Mathematical principles never vary; formulas and equations always exhibit flawless consistency. Consequently, as a tool for studying God's creative handiwork, mathematics helps uncover God's methods of creating.

It is impossible for us to understand creation without God's gift of mathematics, for we would not have the means of measuring His world. Mathematics is a tool to help men rule over the earth under God. All callings in life demand planning, calculating, and evaluating in order to carry out our God-given responsibilities. Mathematics plays an important role, whether it be in business, medicine, engineering, art, science, etc. Therefore, the Christian student should master this wonderful gift to advance Christ's kingdom on Earth.

A Biblical View of Science

Science is the study of God's creation. The facts of creation can be properly understood only by looking at them through the lens of Scripture. By studying science as God's creation the student learns to see God's awesome power, the beauty of His handiwork and design reflected in every creature. Because creation was brought into existence by God's wisdom, and man was created as a part of it, he is called to understand and subdue it for His glory. In Eden God assigned man his task of ruling over the animals and plants, and keeping the earth. Under God's authority, he is to cultivate, care for, and develop each aspect of the world for God's glory. Adam pursued scientific education when he learned to cultivate the soil, plant and dress the trees and vegetation, study the animals, and give each a special name that described them.

To rule over the earth as God commanded, the student must similarly acquire an organized and systematic scientific knowledge. By studying both God's physical laws and His creatures, students will learn to apply this knowledge in accordance with His holy will. As they grow in their knowledge and appreciation of each new discovery about God's world, they should acknowledge that Jehovah is the One who made it and learn to subdue and care for creation in the right way. To do this, the study of science must be subject to the Word of God. Creation must never be seen as something independent of its Creator, about which men can study without reference to Him. Otherwise the student may fall into the trap of the evolutionary worldview and "what is falsely called knowledge" (1 Timothy 6:20).

A Biblical View of Health and Physical Education

The purpose of health and physical education is to cultivate our bodies to the glory of God. The human body has been created by God, and as His creature the student must learn the importance of taking care of it. A healthy body enables one to diligently serve God and perform the duties He commands. Therefore, principles of proper diet, exercise, and rest should be taught for maintaining good health to the glory of God.

Physical education also helps prepare students for responsible leadership and effective work. Students should be taught to play and labor for God's glory—not our own. Due to sin, people are naturally inclined toward laziness. Consequently, physical exercise and sports, when combined with sanctification, can play an important part in developing self-discipline. Through competition students are taught the importance of playing by the rules, accepting direction from those in authority, using skills in harmony with others, and being gracious in victory as well as in defeat.

A Biblical View of Geography

For man to rule over the earth as God has commanded, he must have a practical knowledge of geography. The study of geography must begin with the Holy Bible. Here God reveals that the earth consists of separate but interrelated parts which form a unified whole. During the worldwide flood in the days of Noah, the surface and appearance of the earth was greatly changed. With this important knowledge, the student can properly study the great continents and oceans, their particular characteristics, their many natural resources, the variety of climates and weather patterns, and God's ingenious ecological balance over all the earth.

We also learn in Scripture the origin of the nations, how God divided mankind at the Tower of Babel. It was here that God confused man's language and laid the basis for the nations. The student is then able to properly study the geographical circumstances of the various nations, both ancient and modern. He studies their locations, their natural resources, physical environments, and general climates as planned by God. He learns how these physical traits affect the nations' economies, their position in world trade, their military defense capabilities, and their independence of—or dependence upon—other nations. The study of geography plays an important role for Christian students as they learn about the worldwide advance of the kingdom of God, and how they may help promote Christian missions to every nation and land.

A Biblical View of History

The Bible clearly reveals that God is the Lord of history. He governs all nations and peoples by means of His providence. He acts indirectly and directly in history through blessings and judgments upon the earth (Deuteronomy 28). The prophecies recorded in Scripture, many of which have been fulfilled, demonstrate that history has not only been planned by God but proceeds according to His purpose. For this reason all history—ancient, medieval, and modern—must be seen as the sovereign rule of God over the affairs of men. All men and nations are accountable to Him. The lessons of history warn students that God's curse on unfaithfulness and His blessing on faithfulness will surely come to pass.

A proper understanding of history is built around the key events of creation, man's fall into sin, the cross of Christ, and the return of Christ. Creation sets the stage for history. With Adam's sin, history becomes a conflict between the children of light and the children of darkness. Because God's plan is to sum up all things in Christ (Ephesians 1:10), history has one purpose. Consequently its meaning and interpretation must be understood in terms of Christ. History is more than a chronicle of names, dates, places, and events. History is the study of the moral or covenantal relationship between God and man in time. Its focus centers on the redemptive work of Christ and how He is building His church. All earlier events must look forward to the cross. All later events must

be viewed as the hand of God directing history toward the final victory of the risen Christ at the end of the age.

History studies should focus on the unfolding of world history, with a special emphasis on the shaping of Western culture and its global influence by God's providence. The studies should also include the efforts of past Christians to apply God's Word to individual nations. Students should be equipped to study the vain attempts of apostate men to build the kingdom of man. Those who have attempted to destroy Christ and His Kingdom—in order to restore pagan ideas in the civil, ecclesiastical, and academic disciplines—will have their lives and works evaluated by the Bible. This comparison will help us as we work by God's grace to restore His Word to our lives, families, nations, and cultures in obedience to Genesis 1:26–28, as modified by Matthew 28:19–20. God's people must diligently work and "occupy," as they advance His kingdom on earth through the gospel for His honor and glory.

A Biblical View of Society

Biblical sociology (social studies) begins with God, who exists in an eternal relationship between the Persons of the Trinity. Because the Bible stresses both God's unity and plurality as equally ultimate, we find that it does not place the human individual or the corporate society above each other. Thus Christianity has the only solution to the problems of humanism as it careens between individualism and collectivism.

In His infinite wisdom, God instituted the fundamental social relationship—the family—at creation. From this basic institution, all other social orders have developed according to His providence. He ordained the state, the church, and the family. Each social sphere is directly responsible to God and each has rights that must function within the sphere of authority given to it by Him. These coordinate rights and responsibilities have been clearly marked out in His Holy Law.

The Bible also provides social facts which should be taught. For example, the social structures of the Old Testament covenant community of Israel demonstrate God's purpose for each, and contrasts them with pagan society. A biblical presentation of the social order is needed to address effectively the current corruption of society. Biblical law provides the tools for analyzing the various social structures of different nations and peoples.

Having analyzed God's original order and the perversion of the order by apostate man, the student should be led to see God's provision for an alternate society. What sin has distorted in the social order established by God, He restores by His grace. Students should be instructed in how Christ and His redemption not only restore the relationship between God and man but, as a result, the social relationships between men, women, children, races, and nations. The Christian family and the Christian community—the church—should be presented as the alternate society in the midst of chaos.

A Biblical View of Government

The study of government (political science) and politics must be grounded in the Word of God. In studying civil law and government we need God's infallible standards in order to distinguish justice from injustice. Because civil government enacts laws, it is concerned with deciding right and wrong. Right and wrong, however, have to do with morality, and morality is religious. This means that civil government, by its very nature, is a religious institution.

The Old Testament reveals God's system of law for civil government. At Mount Sinai, through His prophet Moses, God gave to Israel an entire system of civil law and government. The passages following the Decalogue reveal a complete system of law with due process, a federal system of government with three branches at each level, and separation of powers with a system of checks and balances.

The student who learns this system has the proper criterion by which to analyze human governments of the past and present. By using God's perfect law as the standard, political orders can be analyzed as to their structure, laws, and policies. This knowledge will provide the student with understanding necessary for intelligent Christian voting and stimulate him to promote a responsible government regulated by God's Law.

A Biblical View of Economics

God is the possessor of the earth, the source of all wealth. He owns it, and gives it to whomever He wills. He also ordained laws to govern human economics. God has given men the right to own private property, the right to choose an occupation, the right to make a profit, and the right to decide how earnings should be spent. Yet because God owns all things, the student should be taught to exercise these rights as God's steward.

According to Scripture, it is not the duty of civil government to regulate the economy except as it regards the enforcement of God's law against stealing. God's Law affirms the right of private property and profit from labor. To exercise these God-given rights, Scripture provides guidelines for an economic system that glorifies God and shows charity toward the needs of others. Such an economic system is based upon hard work, competition, and the risks of the marketplace. These factors compel sellers to use their skills and economic resources more carefully, which produces a higher quality of goods and services at very reasonable prices. The proper role of civil government is to serve God as a referee, praising good and punishing evil in the marketplace in terms of God's Law.

Wealth is not just a result of economic shrewdness. Economic prosperity is possible only by God's blessing upon the lawful use of labor and profit. Productive harmony in the marketplace is possible only through the grace of God which enables men to obey His law in their hearts and minds. To the extent that men understand and obey God's Law in the economic realm—that is, when Christianity has a significant bearing on economic life—men will respect each other's property; refuse to steal from or cheat one another; abide by contracts; and, when in charge of a corporation or elected to public office, they will not use their power to amass wealth for their own selfish ends.

A Biblical View of Culture, Art, and Technology

The arts and technology are gifts given to men by the Holy Spirit. When an artist paints a picture, a musician composes a song, an architect designs a building, or an engineer designs a machine, each is using his God-given talent. Every gift should be used to reflect the wisdom of its Creator and imitate the beauty and usefulness of His creative work. The humanistic worldview sees culture, art, and technology as existing only for self-expression, human enjoyment, and selfish vanity. The non-Christian uses culture as a way to revolt against God and glorify himself. He thinks that he can create out of nothing something totally original. When man creates, he is not creating something absolutely new, but merely discovering a potentiality which has existed from the beginning. Its proper use becomes a blessing from God for the benefit of men, while its misuse becomes a curse for the destruction of men.

Because the arts and technology create works that express thought and emotion, they exert a moral influence on one's behavior. The arts and technology can be powerful forms of religious fellowship; *religious* because thoughts, emotions, and actions are always moral, and *fellowship* because of the sharing between artist and audience. For the Christian, this imposes a serious responsibility. It means we are not to enjoy art and technology which promotes thoughts, emotions, and behavior contrary to the Word of God. The Scripture says, "… what communion has light with darkness?" (2 Corinthians 6:14). Instead, the student should be taught to enjoy art and produce technology that reflects the glory of God's creation and ministers to others. The student is to develop his talents in harmony with God's truth and law. Furthermore, the Christian should use both the arts and technology, either directly or indirectly, to promote the Gospel of Jesus Christ and thereby promote a biblical understanding of God's world. In so doing, the student will learn how to employ his skills to advance the kingdom of God on earth for His honor and glory.

Teaching Method: Making Disciples of Christ

Education is part of Christ's Great Commission to disciple the nations. The Bible tells parents that they have a moral responsibility before God to bring up their children in the discipline and instruction of the Lord (Ephesians 6:4). The word *discipline* means to train, and the word *instruct* means to teach. Education thus includes both instruction as well as discipline. Therefore, as teachers labor to nurture, instruct, and discipline students, their central task is to make disciples of Christ.

For a biblical curriculum to be profitable, it is necessary for the teacher to practice a biblical method of teaching. Both the mind and the will of the student need to be trained and brought into subjection to God's authority. The teacher should pray and work to the end that the student's reasoning will submit to God's authority. The mind needs to be trained to submit to Scripture, and to resist the temptation of leaning on one's own understanding. False ways of thinking need to be rebuked and the mind brought to humility before God. The student must become a fool that he might become wise (1 Corinthians 3: 18).

Not only should the student be taught to reason in a consistent, biblical, organized manner, but to exercise proper biblical discipline to reach the goal. By warning against unbelief, rebellion, and the spirit of this age, the teacher seeks to train the student to become a disciple of Christ. Parents should train their children morning, noon, and night, as they instruct them in biblical truth. Training includes regular discipline to help students stay on the right path and learn godly habits. Christian training should be the same at home, at school, at church, and

at play. In this way, the student learns that God's Word is to be believed and obeyed consistently, everywhere, and at all times. Otherwise, he will learn to be inconsistent in his behavior before God and man. In short, he will grow to be a hypocrite.

The Goal of Christian Education

To Glorify and Enjoy God

The purpose of Christian education is not primarily to meet human needs or develop human potential, but preeminently to labor to the greater glory of God, the honor of the name of Christ, and promote the development of His kingdom. In a word, the ultimate goal of Christian education is to glorify God and enjoy Him forever. It means that we are to serve Him in every area of life and calling. This takes place when the student learns to fear God and trust Christ so that he will think and act biblically. For this reason, true Christian education must be God-centered: *ad majorem Dei gloriam*—for the greater glory of God.

God created man for the joy of communion with Himself. Therefore, one's joy and fulfillment in life is not to be found in himself or in the world in which he lives, but in loving communion with his Creator. As students learn to glorify God and live for Christ, they will have true enjoyment in life. Without holiness there is no happiness. As the student grows in the knowledge of creation, and discovers the wonders that God has made, he should be taught to enjoy and praise the One who made it. Each new discovery should lead him to acknowledge that God has made us and all things. If education is to train the child for life, then the chief end of man must be constantly kept in view.

To Fear God and Trust in Christ

The fear of the Lord is the beginning of wisdom. To fear the Lord means to take what He says seriously. When education begins with the fear of God, it promotes respect for God's authority as expressed in His Word and Law as the foundation for learning. With reverential awe, the student will approach schoolwork seriously, attempting to do his best. This is absolutely necessary for the student's proper attitude in education.

Since the fear of the Lord is necessary to glorify Him, and without faith it is impossible to please Him, the student needs to come to a saving faith in Christ before he can think and act biblically. The first American college, Harvard, established this standard: "Let every student be plainly instructed and earnestly pressed to consider well, what the main end of his life and studies is, to know God and Jesus Christ, which is eternal life, and therefore to lay Christ in the bottom, as the only foundation of all sound knowledge and learning. And seeing the Lord only gives wisdom, let every one seriously set himself to prayer in secret to seek it of Him." Christian teachers should, by their instruction, discipline, and godly example, pray that the Lord may be pleased to use their teaching as a means to effectually call students unto Christ.

To Reason according to a Biblical Worldview

In every area of study, Christian home educators should train their children to understand God's perspective and think His thoughts after Him. To do this, they must grow in their knowledge of the Word of God and learn the mind of Christ. They must learn to reason in terms of biblical truth, and develop a truly consistent biblical worldview. By godly instruction and precept, through the inculcation of scriptural wisdom, students are to develop their God-created minds unto Christian maturity. They must be taught how to rightly discern and judge all things in the light of Scripture. Christian education fails if it does not instill the pattern of thinking after God's words and logic.

If a student learns to think in terms of himself or the creature, his decisions regarding right and wrong, truth and error, reality and fantasy, will be humanistic or naturalistic. Without realizing it, he will be acting as his own god, determining for himself good and evil (Genesis 3:5).

To Love and Serve God and Our Neighbor

Knowledge for the sake of knowledge is useless and leads to intellectual arrogance, but *true knowledge must be used practically to advance the Kingdom of God for His glory.* Christian education therefore uses knowledge to glorify God and minister to others. Biblical ethics demands that education must not be used as a means of self-glorification. Students should learn to obey and serve God more fully so that they may minister to others more effectively. Students must learn to walk in the truth, and through faith manifest the fruit of the Spirit in good works. Thus, after coming to faith in Christ and developing a biblical worldview, the development of strong godly character and a lifestyle of service is most necessary. In fact, godliness is necessary for a proper understanding of the truth.

To love and serve God is an empty lie if there is no heart to serve others. Christian education aims to train men and women who love God in both word and deed, and express this love in ministering to others. One's vocation must be seen as part of this moral responsibility. It is not merely the obtaining of a paycheck, but to serve God and our neighbor. This love includes loving what God loves, and hating what God hates. Loving others does not mean that we will embrace all faults and lies in others, but it does mean that we will love them by ministering Christ to them.

Biblical education is devoted also to the development of the student's spiritual, academic, and physical welfare. Each student has received talents, opportunities, and blessings from his Maker. Christian education seeks not merely to develop one's potential, but to assist the student to find his place, meaning, purpose, and responsibilities in the plan of God. Christian home educators seek to help prepare their students to fulfill God's calling for their lives, that they might labor to advance the kingdom of God on earth for His glory. Christian education can help determine God's call on their lives, and equip them with skills and knowledge by which they can glorify God effectively. As students better understand God's Word and how to apply it to God's world, they will be able to take dominion in their calling under Jesus Christ. Christian home educators are dedicated to train up their children in the way they should go, so that when they are old they will not depart from it (Proverbs 22:6).

Understanding Education

by Tom Parent

The Three Stages of Maturity

To help us to fulfill our responsibilities before God as parents, it is important for us to understand how to effectively train our children in the way of the Lord. To effectively train our children, we must not only have the proper knowledge ourselves, we must also be able to communicate it to them.

One important way for parents to improve communication is to realize that, from birth until adulthood, children pass through the following three stages of maturity: the *curiosity stage*, *analytical stage*, and *expressive stage*.

The Curiosity Stage

The *curiosity stage* is primarily from birth to eight years of age, although it does extend somewhat beyond this. At this stage, the powers of logic are not yet predominant, which makes reasoning difficult and unenjoyable. Learning by heart, on the other hand, is easy and fun—when it is presented in the proper way.

Children at this level readily memorize the shapes and appearance of things. There is a certain fascination for strange-sounding words, the chanting of rhymes and poems, and even the reciting of numbers on car license plates. At this level, children delight in detail and the mere accumulation of things, a sort of learning for learning's sake.

The Analytical Stage

The *analytical stage* approximately begins at age nine, but does not really take hold until about the eighth grade. Its tell-tale signs are answering back, correcting one's elders, and the challenging of others with clever riddles and thought-provoking problems.

At this stage, students' minds are geared for logical analysis. Memorization of details and learning for learning's sake is sheer boredom. They have developed a questioning attitude and a healthy sense of contradiction. Here students are more interested in making sense out of details than in mere details themselves.

Formerly, the learning of facts was important. Now, the logic of facts is important. Therefore, the teacher must instruct in a way that encourages analysis, debate, and constructive criticism of the subject matter at hand. If the teacher continues using the approach of learning for learning's sake, students will become bored and disinterested.

The Expressive Stage

The third and final stage is the *expressive stage*. This stage often begins around age fifteen and is popularly known as the "difficult years." Students at this age usually tend to be self-centered and often feel that they are misunderstood. These are the restless years in which teens yearn to express themselves and try to achieve independence.

At this stage there is the beginning of self-expression and creativeness, a need to take everything that has been learned and "put it all together." There is a deliberate eagerness to select one vocation in preference to all others. Students instinctively realize that logic itself is not enough and that there is a real need for an overall view of life; a view which will pull together everything that has been learned into a consistent body of thought.

At the analytical stage, teachers concentrated on developing the students' skills in each particular subject area. At the expressive stage, however, teachers concentrate on training students to use their individual skills together, harmoniously, in preparation for a practical life in the outside world.

Application to Teaching

If we take these three stages of maturity and apply them to the overall grade levels, we can see a pattern for teaching:

Stage of Maturity	Grade Level
Curiosity	K–3
Intermediate Phase	4–6
Analytical	7–9
Expressive	10–12

Kindergarten through third grade is the *curiosity stage* in which we see the student learning for learning's sake. Here students collect the fundamental facts and truths about life.

Grades four through six encompass the *intermediate phase*, beginning at age nine, where the curiosity stage begins to fade out and the analytical stage begins to fade in. These grades are not only transitional but also preparatory for the analytical stage of development. In grades seven through nine, students are in the *analytical stage* and want to know the logic of facts. At this stage, the meaning of things is all-important.

Finally, in the *expressive stage*, grades ten through twelve (and into college), students need to "put it all together" in order to experience a sense of purpose and direction to life. This does not mean that facts and logic are to be ignored at this stage. On the contrary, they are to be continued. The emphasis, however, is to complete the job of education by bringing all previous learning together for the purpose of practical application in the outside world.

If students have been taught properly at the curiosity and analytical stages, they will be able to express themselves constructively and to develop a practical approach to life. But if the necessary training and skills are missing, they will enter the expressive stage with feelings of inferiority and frustration, as they realize that they are unable to cope with the real world.

The Three Tools of Learning

Running parallel with the three stages of maturity are the following three tools of learning: the *particulars*—the learning of particular facts; *systems*—seeing facts brought together into organized and logical systems; and the *interrelation of systems*—seeing how systems are brought together for use in a practical way.

To better understand how these three tools of learning work, let's begin with an example with which many of us are familiar, namely, the automobile. To get started, let's pretend that we are in a large room with a pile of auto parts lying in the center of the floor. In walks a master mechanic who starts to sort out the various parts into smaller piles.

As he finishes the sorting process, he walks over to one of the smaller piles and says to us, "These are the parts for the carburetor." He then shows us each of the parts (the particulars), giving us their correct names and describing their functions, while proceeding to assemble them into a carburetor (which is a system).

Our mechanic repeats this same procedure with the ignition system, the transmission system, the exhaust system, and so on until all of the various systems of the automobile have been assembled. With this accomplished, he finally connects all of the systems together (the interrelation of systems) until we have before us a fully assembled automobile.

In teaching us about the automobile, our master mechanic used the three tools of learning. First, he described the various parts (the particulars), giving us their names and explaining their functions. Second, he assembled these various parts, step-by-step, into their respective systems (carburetor, ignition, etc.).

Finally, he interconnected all of the individual systems, (the inter-relation of systems) producing an automobile.

If we apply these same three steps to the teaching of *reading*, we should have equally successful results. For example, the twenty-six letters of the alphabet are the particulars. Of the twenty-six letters, some are vowels and some consonants. Both vowels and consonants have special jobs to do.

As the young student learns the alphabet, he learns that the vowels and the consonants have individual and distinct sounds. In other words, he learns to identify the symbols that he sees with the sounds that he hears. As he masters this process, he is ready for the next step which is the assembling of the vowels and the consonants (particulars) together into words (systems). From here he learns that words are used together to form a sentence (the inter-relation of systems), which expresses a thought.

When this basic foundational work is completed, our student is at the language grammar level and the three tools of learning apply here also. At this level, the different kinds of sentences now become the particulars. The student is taught that there are descriptive sentences, declarative sentences, interrogatory sentences, exclamatory sentences, and so forth, which he is trained to see as expressing various kinds of thoughts and feelings.

His next step then, is to learn how to use these different kinds of sentences (particulars), bringing them together to form paragraphs (systems). Gradually, the student learns to use paragraphs (systems) skillfully in the development of stories and essays (the interrelation of systems).

The following outline will help you to understand the pattern of the three tools of learning in *reading* and *grammar*:

	Reading	Grammar
Particulars	vowels and consonants	sentences
Systems	words	paragraphs
Interrelation of Systems	sentences	stories and essays

The teaching of vowels and consonants to form words is known as phonics. The main reason for the serious reading problem in many of the public schools is the lack of intensive phonics as a first and fundamental step. In skipping this first step, the student is trained to memorize whole words (systems) instead of learning to sound out words by means of their particulars. By grades four and five, the memory load on many students becomes too great. With the ability to read seriously deficient, the student fails in other subjects as well. These children are then labeled as "learning disabled" and either left to make it on their own or placed in special remedial programs. The emotional damage and the loss of self-confidence suffered by these children is considerable.

For true education to take place, all three tools are essential. Regardless of what subject is being taught, the basic mechanism remains the same. This is true because we live in a world created by God. And in His world, there are fundamental truths which never change.

To further illustrate the application of these tools of learning, we will consider the subject of *history*. History begins with the study of people as individuals and groups (the particulars) interacting with each other, at a specific place in time, to produce an event (a system). Historians study a certain series of events (the interrelation of systems) which goes to make up the history of an individual or a group or a nation. For example, in *American history*, we might study various individuals (Samuel Adams, George Washington, Patrick Henry, King George III) and groups (the English Parliament, the Mercantilists, and the American colonists—Patriots and Tories) which interacted together to produce an event, namely the American War for Independence (1775–1783).

Using the same approach (particular individuals and groups interacting to

form an event), we would then
study other events such as the
Constitutional Convention in
Philadelphia (1787), the War
of 1812, the enactment of the
Monroe Doctrine (1823), the
Mexican War (1846–1848),
the War Between the States
(1861–1865) and so on.
This series of events makes
up what we call American history (the interrelation of systems).

The following table illustrates the pattern of the three tools
of learning in history:

Particulars	individuals and groups
Systems	interacting to form an event
Interrelation of Systems	a series of interrelated events

With regard to the study of *geography*, the three tools of learning
apply equally well in understanding weather patterns. In one system, the sun, the air, and the ocean waters are the particulars.
During the day, the sun's rays heat both the ocean waters (increasing the rate of water evaporation) and the air over the ocean (caus-
ing it to expand). The expanded air soaks up the evaporating
water and, being warm, rises to meet the cooler air above. As the
warm moist air mingles with the cooler air, the water vapors con-
dense forming clouds.

In another system, the particulars are the sun, the land surface,
and the ocean surface. The land surface, being denser than water,
heats up faster and, as a result, the warmer land air rises more rapidly than the comparatively cooler air over the ocean. Because the
land air moves upward faster, it draws the moisturized ocean air
inland. Consequently, the temperature difference between the land
surface and the ocean surface creates wind currents. The interrelation of these two simple weather systems produces a basic weather

pattern. Working together, the two systems bring rain and snow to the various land areas of the earth.

In the study of *mathematics*, we again see the three tools of learning applied. The particulars are the individual numbers which are used in organized systems such as addition, subtraction, multiplication, and division. The interrelation of these systems takes place when two or more systems (addition and subtraction or multiplication and division) are used to solve a specific mathematical problem. This same approach applies to algebra, geometry, trigonometry, and all forms of mathematics.

The list of subjects, however, does not end here. These tools of learning are also used in other areas of study, including physics, chemistry, psychology, sociology, political science, economics, and business management. This shows that the world in which we live is systematic, and therefore organized, which is a powerful argument in favor of creation over evolution. Consequently, since all areas of life can be studied systematically, we must look to the Great Organizer for assistance in understanding His world.

To do this necessitates a working knowledge of the *Bible* where, again, we need to apply the three tools of learning. First, we must study God's Word and learn His various teachings (the particulars). Then we need to organize these teachings into individual systems or doctrines (a catechism). Finally, these individual doctrines are brought together (the interrelation of systems) to give us a picture or view of God and both the world and ourselves in relation to God.

This worldview becomes our basis and point of reference for all that we study. Consequently, the Christian sees history as a series of events directed by God toward a predetermined goal. Science is the study of God's organized control over nature (the laws of physics, the laws of chemistry, etc.). Both language and mathematics are seen as essential tools for measuring and defining the various particulars and systems of God's world. All study and all learning have their meaning and purpose in relation to the Creator who made all things. In other words, the Bible provides the context from which all facts derive their meaning.

The Three Levels of Learning

We will now examine the *three levels of learning* which have to do with the curriculum.

First, we discussed the three stages of maturity:

Curiosity Stage	ages birth–8
Analytical Stage	ages 9-14
Expressive Stage	ages 15–20

The three stages of maturity are the foundation for the *three levels of learning* in the curriculum (K–12 and into college). The three levels of learning consist of:

Learning the facts	birth–6th grade
Understanding the facts	7th–9th grades
Using the facts	10th grade–college

The *first level of learning* (learning the facts) is primarily from kindergarten through sixth grade. Because children are at the curiosity stage in maturity, the first level concentrates on learning facts and information.

As the maturity of the student progresses to the analytical stage, he enters the *second level of learning*. Primarily in grades seven through nine, the student concentrates on the logic and meaning of what he has learned. As things begin to make sense, facts and information become knowledge; that is, we cannot truly know something until we understand it.

For example, in the study of *history*, at the *first level*, the student learns names, dates, places, and events. The emphasis here is on learning the facts. At the *second level* (grades 7–9), the student concentrates on analyzing the facts in order to understand the causes and effects of certain events and to determine whether they were good or bad. At this level, the student wants to know: "Was the behavior of this statesman justified?" "What were the effects of certain laws?" "What are the arguments for and against this or that form of government?" It is this systematic approach to history which provides the necessary foundation for the *third level of learning*, namely, the practical study of civil government and economics. Without a proper understanding of civil government and economics, the preservation of a free nation is impossible.

With the study of *mathematics*, the *first level* has to do with the learning of specific numbers and their use in addition, subtraction, multiplication, division, fractions, and decimals. The first level deals with specifics ($2 + 2 = 4$, $3 \times 6 = 18$, etc.). At the *second level*, the student goes beyond the specifics of mathematics into the logic or understanding of mathematics. Through the study of algebra (the *third level*), the student learns to see addition, subtraction, multiplication, and division as functional formulas. For example, $2 + 2 = 4$ is really $a + b = c$ (one quantity added to another quantity equals the sum total of both). Likewise, $3 \times 6 = 18$ is actually $x \times y = z$ (one quantity multiplied by another quantity equals the multiplied combination of both).

The same is true of *geometry*. At the *first level of learning*, the student learns the various geometrical shapes (squares, triangles, rectangles, etc.). At the *second level*, the student learns that these various shapes have logical patterns (the sum of the measures of the angles of a triangle is $180°$; a circle is the set of all points in a plane that are equidistant from one point in the plane; etc.).

Both algebra and geometry, and other forms of advanced math, provide the necessary foundation for the study of physics and chemistry which, in turn, are the basis for training in electronics, industrial engineering, nuclear physics, architectural design, and other practical areas of life.[4]

Thus we see that the *three levels of learning* correspond to the *three stages of maturity*; curiosity stage (K–6th grade) = learning the facts; analytical stage (7th–9th grade) = understanding the facts (knowledge); and expressive stage (10th grade–college) = using the facts (wisdom).

Summary

The *first level of learning* involves the gradual accumulation of basic facts and information in each of the fundamental disciplines (math, reading, writing, spelling, grammar, science, history, etc.), forming a foundation for thought and action.

The *second level* consists of understanding the logic of each of these disciplines, resulting in knowledge. At the same time, the student learns how to apply this knowledge by developing skills in each of these disciplines.

In the *third level*, all of this individualized knowledge, in each of the subjects, is brought together into an overall consistent body of thought, which is essential if the student is to learn how to use, as a whole, all of the individual skills he has developed. In other words, this level is the culmination of thought and skill, resulting in self-sufficiency under God and the ability to successfully exercise dominion (Christian stewardship) in the real world. The key to accomplishing this, however, is the Word of God, and, in the next section, we will examine how the Holy Scriptures bear on curriculum.

---

4. The study of physics and chemistry is not always necessary for the third level. For example, the study of accounting, economics, and business management, as well as auto mechanics, carpentry, and masonry, are practical expressions of the *third level*.

How Should a Child Be Trained?

By J. C. Ryle

> Bring them up in the training and admonition of the Lord.
>
> *Ephesians 6:4*

How little is this text regarded! We live in days when there is a mighty zeal for education, new schools rising on all sides, new systems and new books for training the young, of every description. These things may well give rise to great searchings of heart. The subject is one that should come home to every conscience; there is hardly a household that it does not touch.

This is preeminently a subject in which we can see the faults of our neighbors more clearly than our own. We need to suspect our own judgment. I have sometimes been perfectly astonished at the slowness of sensible Christian parents to allow that their children are in the fault or deserve blame.

Come now, and let us have before us a few hints, words in season. Reject them not because they are blunt and simple.

First, if we would train our children wisely we must train them according to the Word of God.

Remember, children are born with a decided bias toward evil. Therefore, if we let them choose for themselves, they are certain to choose wrong.

The mother cannot tell what the tender infant may grow up to be, tall or short, weak or strong, wise or foolish; he may be any of these things, or not—it is all uncertain. But one thing the mother can say with certainty; he will have a corrupt and sinful heart. It is natural for us to do wrong. "Foolishness," God says, "is bound up in the heart of a child" (Proverbs 22:15a). "[A] child left to himself brings shame to his mother" (Proverbs 29:15b).

If, then, we would deal wisely with our child, we must not leave him to the guidance of his own will. We must think for him, judge for him, just as we would for one weak and blind; but we should not give him up to his own wayward tastes and inclinations. It must not be his likings and wishes that are consulted. He knows not yet what is good for his mind and soul, any more than what is good for his body. Do not let him decide what he shall eat, and what he shall drink and how he shall be clothed. What shameful scenes at the table might be avoided if parents would seek divine wisdom as to what is best to put on the child's plate.

If we do not consent to this first divine principle of training, it is useless to read any further. Self-will is almost the first thing that appears in the child's mind; and it must be our first step to resist it. The best horse in the world had to be broken.

Train up your child with all tenderness, affection and patience.

I do not mean that you should spoil him, but I do mean that you should let him see that you love him. Kindness, gentleness, long-suffering, forbearance, patience, sympathy, a willingness to enter into childish troubles, a readiness to take part in childish joys—these are the cords by which a child may be led most easily; these are the clues you must follow if you would find the way to his heart.

Sternness and severity of manner chill them and throw them back. It shuts up their hearts, and you will weary yourself to find the door. But let them see that you have an affectionate feeling towards them; that you are really desirous to make them happy and to do them good; that if you punish them it is intended for their profit.

Children are weak and tender creatures, and as such they need patient and considerate treatment. We must handle them delicately, like sensitive plants, lest by rough fingering we do them more harm than good.

We must not expect all things at once. We must remember what they are and teach them what they are able to bear. Their understandings are like narrow-necked vessels; we must pour in the wine of knowledge gradually, or much of it will be spilled and lost. Line upon line, and precept upon precept, here a little and there a little, must be our rule. Truly there is need of patience in training a child, for without it nothing can be done.

Nothing will compensate for the absence of tenderness and love. You may set before your children their duty; command, threaten, punish, reason; but if affection be wanting in your treatment, your labor will be in vain. Love is the one grand secret of successful training. Anger and harshness may frighten, but will not persuade the child that you are right; and if he sees you often out of temper, you will soon cease to have his respect. Fear puts an end to openness of manner; fear leads to concealment; fear sows the seed of hypocrisy, and leads to many a lie. There is a mine of truth in the apostle's words to the Colossians, "Fathers, do not provoke your children, lest they become discouraged" (Colossians 3:21).

Train your children diligently, remembering the importance of right training.

The habits that are formed by children in their early years will likely stay with them their whole lives. Our character takes the form of that mold into which our first years are cast, not forgetting, of course, what the grace of God can do for those who look to Him. In many respects, we are made what we are by training.

God gives our children a mind that will receive impressions like moist clay, and to trust our word rather than a stranger's. In short, He gives each parent a golden opportunity of doing them good. See that the opportunity be not neglected and thrown away.

I know that you cannot convert your child. I know well that they who are born again are born, not of the will of man, but of God. But I also know that God says expressly, "Bring them up in the training and admonition of the Lord," and He never laid a command on man which He would not give man grace to perform. The path of obedience is the way of blessing. We have only to do as the servants were commanded at the marriage feast in Cana, to fill the water pots with water, and we may safely leave it to the Lord to turn that water to wine.

Ever bear in mind that the soul of your child is the first thing to be considered.

Precious, no doubt, are these little ones in our eyes; but if we love them we will think often of their souls. No interest will weigh with us so much as their eternal welfare. No part of them should be so dear to us as that part which will never die. The world, with all its glory, shall pass away; but the spirit which dwells in those little creatures, whom we love so well, shall outlive them all, and whether in happiness or misery (to speak as a man) will depend on us. This is the thought that should be uppermost in our minds, in all we do for our children. How will this affect their souls?

To pet, pamper, and indulge our child, as if this world was all he had to look to, and this life the only season for happiness—to do this is not true love, but cruelty. Nor is it fidelity to Christ.

A faithful Christian must be no slave to fashion, if he would train his child for the Lord. He must not be content to do things merely because they are the custom of the world, and especially the Christian should avoid the popular but unwarranted traditions, such as "Halloween" and "Easter" (Galatians 4:10; Romans 12:2). Nor is it protecting them by allowing them to read the vain "comics" and books of a questionable sort, merely because everybody reads them. What can bring the world into the home more than television? He must not be ashamed to hear his training called singular and strange. What if it is? The time is short—the fashion of this world passeth away. He that has trained his children for heaven rather than for earth—for God rather than man—he is that parent that will be called wise at the last. "[H]e who does the will of God abides forever" (I John 2:17).

Train your child in the knowledge of the Bible.

We cannot make our children love the Bible. None but the Holy Spirit can give them a heart to delight in the Word. But we can make our children acquainted with the Bible; and be sure they cannot be acquainted with that blessed Book too soon or too well. Let the simple Bible be everything in the training of their souls; and let all other books take second place.

See that your children read the Bible reverently; it is in truth the Word of God. See that they read it regularly.

Tell them of sin, its guilt, its consequences, its power, its vileness—we will find they can comprehend something of this. Tell them of the Lord Jesus Christ, His love, and His work for our salvation—His cross, His shed blood, His resurrection, ascension and soon coming again. You will find there is something not beyond them in all this.

Train them to a habit of prayer.

Parents, if you love your children, do all that lies in your power to train them up to a habit of prayer. Show them how to begin. Tell them what to say. Encourage them to persevere. Remind them if they become careless and slack about prayer. As the first steps in any undertaking are always the most important, so is the manner in which our children's prayers are prayed, a point which deserves our closest attention. Few seem to know they get into the habit of saying their prayers in a hasty, careless, and irreverent manner. Reader, if you love your children, I charge you, do not let the seedtime of a prayerful habit pass away.

Train them to assemble in a scriptural way with the people of God.

Tell them that where the Lord's people are gathered together in His name, there the Lord Jesus is present in a special manner, and that those who absent themselves must expect, like the apostle Thomas, to miss a blessing— "not forsaking the assembling of ourselves together, as is the manner of some" (Hebrews 10:25a).

Do not allow them to grow up with a habit of deciding whether or not they want to go to the meetings.

Neither do I like to see what I call a "young people's corner" in an assembly. They often catch habits of inattention and irreverence there which it takes years to unlearn, if ever they are unlearned at all. What I like to see is a whole family sitting together. "We will go with our young and our old; with our sons and our daughters, … for we must hold a feast to the LORD" (Exodus 10:9).

Nor should we lightly esteem the Lord's Day by turning it into a day of recreation and self-gratification.

Train them to obey you without always knowing why.

We should teach them to accept everything we require of them as for their good.

I have heard it said by some, that we should require nothing of children which they cannot understand; that we should explain and give a reason for everything we desire them to do. I warn you solemnly against such a notion. I tell you plainly, I think it is an unsound and unscriptural principle. No doubt it is absurd to make a mystery of everything we do, and there are many things which it is well to explain to children, in order that they may see that they are reasonable and wise. But to bring them up with the idea that they must take nothing on trust—that they, with their weak and imperfect understandings, must have the "why" and "wherefore" made clear to them at every step they take—this is indeed a fearful mistake, and likely to have the worst effect on their minds.

Set before them the example of Isaac, in the day when Abraham took him to offer him on Mount Moriah (Genesis 22). He asked his father that single question, "Where is the lamb for a burnt offering?" And he got no answer but this, "God will provide for Himself the lamb." How, or where, or whence, or in what manner, or by what means—all this Isaac was not told; but the answer was enough. He believed that it would be well, because his father said so, and he was content.

Train them to a habit of prompt obedience.

This is an object which it is worth any labor to attain. No habit I suspect has such an influence over our lives as this. Parents, determine to make your children obey you, though it may cost you much trouble and cost them many tears. Let there be no questioning, and reasoning, and disputing, and delaying, and answering again. When you give them a command, let them see plainly that you will have it done. It is the mark of well-trained children that they do whatsoever their parents command them. Where indeed is the honor which Ephesians 6:1 enjoins, if fathers and mothers are not obeyed, cheerfully, willingly, and at once? (Ephesians 6:1–4; Colossians 3:20).

Early obedience has all Scripture on its side. It is said in Abraham's praise that not merely will he train his family, but "he may command his children and his household after him" (Genesis 18:19). It is said of the Lord Jesus Himself, that when He was young He was subject to Mary and Joseph (Luke 2:51). Note how the Apostle Paul names disobedience to parents as one of the bad signs of the last days (2 Timothy 3:2).

Parents, do you wish to see your children happy? Take care, then that you train them to obey when they are spoken to—to do as they are told. Believe me, we are not made for entire independence; we are not fit for it. Even Christ's freemen have a yoke to wear—to "serve the Lord Christ" (Colossians 3:24). Children cannot learn too soon that this is a world in which we are not intended to divinely rule, and that we are never in our right place until we know how to obey. Teach them to obey while young, or else they will be complaining against God all their lives long, with the vain idea of being independent of His control.

You will see many in this day who allow their children to choose and think for themselves long before they are able, and even make excuses for their disobedience, as if it were a thing not to be blamed. To my eyes, a parents always yielding, and a child always having his own way, is a most painful sight; painful because I see God's appointed order of things inverted and turned upside down; painful, because I feel sure the consequence to that child's character in the end will be self-evil and self-conceit.

Train them always to speak the truth, and the whole truth, and nothing but the truth.

God is spoken of as the God of truth. Less than the truth is a lie; evasion, excuse-making, and exaggeration are all halfway houses toward what is false, and ought to be avoided. Encourage them in any circumstance to be straightforward, and whatever it may cost them, to speak the truth.

I urge it also for our own comfort and assistance in all our dealings with them. We will find it a mighty help, indeed, to be always able to trust their word. It will go far to prevent that habit of concealment which so unhappily prevails among children.

Train them to a habit of always redeeming the time.

Idleness is the devil's best friend. It is the surest way to give him an opportunity of doing harm. An idle mind is like an open door and if Satan does not enter in himself by it, it is certain he will throw in something to raise bad thoughts in our souls. We must have our hands filled and our minds occupied with something, or else our imaginations will soon foment and breed mischief. "[T]his was

the iniquity of your sister Sodom: She and her daughter had pride, fullness of food, and abundance of idleness" (Ezekiel 16:49). Verily, I believe that idleness has led to more sin than almost any other habit that could be named. I love to see children active and industrious, and giving their whole heart to all they do.

Train them with a constant fear of overindulgence.

I know well that punishment and correction are disagreeable things. Nothing is more unpleasant than giving pain to those we love, and calling forth their tears. But so long as hearts are what they are, it is vain to suppose, as a general rule, that children can be brought up without correction. Spoiling is a very expressive word and sadly full of meaning. Now it is the shortest way to spoil children to let them have their own way—to allow them to do wrong, and not to punish them for it. Believe me, you must not do it, whatever pain it may cost you, unless you wish to ruin your children's souls.

"He who spares his rod hates his son, but he who loves him disciplines him promptly" (Proverbs 13:24). "Chasten your son while there is hope, and do not set your heart on his destruction" (Proverbs 19:18). "Foolishness is bound up in the heart of a child, but the rod of correction will drive it far from him" (Proverbs 22:15). "Do not withhold correction from a child, for if you beat him with a rod, he will not die. You shall beat him with a rod, and deliver his soul from hell" (Proverbs 23:13, 14). "The rod and reproof give wisdom, but a child left to himself brings shame to his mother.... Correct your son, and he will give you rest; yes, he will give delight to your soul" (Proverbs 29:15, 17).

How strong and forcible are these texts! How melancholy is the fact, that in many Christian families they seem almost unknown! Their children need reproof, but it is hardly ever given; they need correction, but it is hardly ever employed. And yet this book of Proverbs is not obsolete and unfit for the Christian. It is given by inspiration of God, and is very profitable. Surely the believer who brings up his children without attention to its counsel, is making himself wise above that which is written, and greatly errs.

Fathers and mothers, I tell you plainly, if you never punish your children when they are in fault, you are doing them a grievous wrong. I warn you, this is the rock on which the saints of God, in every age, have only too frequently made shipwreck. I would fain persuade you to be wise in time, and keep clear of it. See it in Eli's case. His sons Hophni and Phinehas made themselves vile, and he restrained them not. He gave them no more than a tame and luke-warm reproof, when he ought to have rebuked them sharply. In one word he honored his sons above God. And what was the end of these things? He lived to hear of the death of both of his sons in battle and his own gray hairs were brought down with sorrow to the grave (I Samuel 2:12–34; 3:10–18; 4:11–18).

See, too, the case of David. Who can read without pain, the history of his children and their sins? Remember Amnon's incest, Absalom's murder and proud rebellion, and Adonijah's scheming ambition? In the account of Adonijah, in I Kings 1:6, "his father had not rebuked him at any time by saying, 'Why have you done so?'" There was the foundation of all the mischief. David was an overindulgent father—a father who let his children have their own way; and he reaped according as he had sown.

Parents, I beseech you, for your children's sakes, beware of overin-dulgence. I call on you to remember, it is your first duty to consult their real interest, and not their fancies and likings; to train them, not to humor them; to profit, not merely to please.

You must not give way to every wish and caprice of your child's mind, however much you may love him; you must not let him suppose his will is to be everything, and that he has only to desire a thing and it will be done. Do not, I pray, make your children idols, lest God should take them away, and break your idols, just to convince you of your folly. Learn to say "No" to your children. Show them that you are able to refuse whatever you think is not fit for them. Involvement in certain unrequired school activities and entertainments require firmness lest your children become swept into the current of Satan's allurements.

Show them that you are ready to punish disobedience, and that when you speak of punishment you are not only ready to threaten, but also to perform. Avoid engaging in perpetual threatening. Fewer punishments carried out completely and thoroughly are better than frequent and slight punishments. However, do not allow disobedience to pass unpunished. When disciplining your children becomes needful, it is imperative that the parents stand together in loving cooperation.

Beware of letting small faults pass unnoticed, under the idea "it is a little one." There are no little things in training children; all are important. Little weeds need plucking up as much as any. Leave them alone and they will soon be large. Reader, if you do not trouble with your children when they are young, they will give you trouble when they are old.

Train them, remembering continually how God trains His children.

If you would train your children wisely, mark well how God the Father trains His. He doeth all things well; the plan which He adopts must be light. God's children would tell you, in the long run it was a blessed thing they did not have their way, and that God had done better for them than they could have done for themselves. Yes, and they could tell you, too, that God's dealings had provided more happiness for them than they ever would have obtained themselves.

I ask you to lay to heart the lesson which God's dealings with His people are meant to teach you. Fear not to withhold from your child any thing you think will do him harm, whatever his own wishes may be. This is God's plan. To be indulged perpetually is the way to be made selfish; and selfish people and spoiled children are seldom happy. Reader, be not wiser than God; train your children as He trains His.

Train them, remembering continually the influence of your own example.

There is no substitute for godliness—reality with God in the lives of the parents. Instruction, advice and commands will profit little unless they are backed up by the pattern of your life. Your children will never believe you are in earnest, and really wish them to obey you, so long as your actions contradict your counsel. We little know the force and power of example. Children see our ways, they mark our conduct, they observe our behavior. Never, I believe, does example tell so powerfully as it does in the case of parents and children. Fathers and mothers, do not forget that children learn more by the eye than they do by the ear. What they see has a much stronger effect on their minds than what they are told.

Strive rather to be a living epistle of Christ, such as your children can read, and that plainly. Be an example in words, in temper, in diligence, in temperance, in faith, in kindness, in humility. Do not think your children will practice what they do not see you do. You are their model picture, and they will copy what you are.

Your reasoning and your lecturing, your wise commands, and your good advice—all this they may not understand, but they can understand your life. As you enjoy Christ for yourself, they will believe it is something real. Children are very quick observers, very quick in seeing through hypocrisy, very quick in finding out what you really think and feel, very quick in adopting all your ways and opinions; and you will generally find as the father so is the son.

Train them, remembering continually the power of sin.

This will guard you against unscriptural expectations. It is painful to see how much corruption and evil there is in a young child's heart, and how soon it begins to bear fruit—violent tempers, self-will, pride, sullenness, passion, idleness, selfishness, deceit, cunning, falsehood, hypocrisy, a terrible aptness to learn what is bad, a painful slowness to learn what is good, a readiness to pretend anything in order to gain their own ends. You must not think it strange and unusual that little hearts can be so full of sin. It is the only portion which our father Adam left us; it is that fallen nature with which we come into the world.

Never listen to those who tell you your children are good, and well brought up, and can be trusted. At their very best they want only a spark to set their corruptions ablaze. Parents are seldom too cautious. Remember the natural depravity of your children and take care.

"Cast your bread upon the waters," saith the Spirit, "for you will find it after many days" (Ecclesiastes 11:1). Many children, I doubt not, shall rise up in the day of judgment and bless their parents for good training, who never gave any signs of having profited by it during their parents' lives. Go forward then in faith, and be sure your labor shall not be altogether thrown away. Three times did Elijah stretch himself upon the widow's child before he revived. Take example from him and persevere.

Train with continual prayer for blessing on all you do.

Look upon your children as Jacob did on his; he tells Esau, they are "[t]he children whom God has graciously given your servant" (Genesis 33:5b). Look upon them as Joseph did on his; he told his father, "[t]hey are my sons, whom God has given me" (Genesis 48:9). Count them with the Psalmist to be "a heritage from the LORD." (Psalm 127:3) See how Manoah speaks to the angel about Samson: "What will be the boy's rule of life, and his work?" (Judges 13:12b). Observe how tenderly Job cared for his children's souls; "[H]e would ... offer burnt offerings according to the number of them all," for he said, "'It may be that my sons have sinned and cursed God in their hearts.' Thus Job did regularly" (Job 1:5).

Parents, if you love your children, go and do likewise. You cannot name their names before the mercy seat too often.

Fathers and mothers, you may send your children to the best of schools and give them Bibles, and fill them with head knowledge; but if all this time there is no regular training at home, I tell you plainly, I fear it will go hard in the end with your children's souls.

Children have mixed the bitterest cups that man has ever had to drink. Children have caused the saddest tears that man has ever had to shed. Adam could tell you so; David could tell you so. There are no sorrows on earth like those children have brought upon their parents.

Oh, take heed lest your own neglect should lay up misery for you in your old age.

> Pour out your heart like water before the face of the LORD. Lift up your hands toward Him for the life of your young children.

Lamentations 2:19b

PART 2

The Fundamentals of Christian Homeschooling

The Centrality of the Christian Home in Education

by David Gamble

Homeschooling may not be workable for everyone, but it should be considered. Even if Junior attends a good Christian school, Mom and Dad should teach some things at home. The Christian school is an extension of the Christian home, and the home should never abdicate all of its teaching responsibilities to others, no matter how good and godly they are. Children need to think of Mom and Dad as sources of wisdom, knowledge, and guidance.

Perhaps the classic Scriptural passage concerning Christian education is the sixth chapter of the book of Deuteronomy. After reviewing the Covenant and the Ten Commandments, God calls upon His people to love Him, to hide His words in their hearts, and to teach these things to their children. It should be noted that the home is the central place of learning. It

> *...[Y]ou shall teach them diligently to your children, and shall talk of them when you sit in your house, when you walk by the way, when you lie down, and when you rise up....*
>
> *You shall write them on the doorposts of your house and on your gates.*
>
> *Deuteronomy 6:7, 9*

does not necessarily follow that the home is to be the only place of learning, but the basic importance of the home is unmistakable. Learning should not be separated from the rest of life, nor should it occur exclusively in a special building, nor should it occur only when under the tutelage of a specialist.

The God who created children created the family to nurture them. In Psalm 78:5–8, we see the fathers teaching their children the laws of God, and they in turn teach their children also. This is as it should be. Paul mentions the fatherly functions of exhorting, comforting, and charging in I Thessalonians 2:11. Young Timothy, apparently without the benefit of a believing father, was taught the ways of God by his mother and grandmother. (II Timothy 3:15)

Edith Schaeffer, in her marvelous book, *What is a Family?*, writes the following:

> When we are told in Proverbs 22:6 to 'Train up a child in the way he should go: and when he is old, he will not depart from it,' it is not an admonition to simply 'whack' the child to make him or her obey, nor is it just an admonition to teach that child Scripture as a separate subject. I believe strongly it is a command to train the whole person—intellectually, spiritually, culturally, emotionally—in things of creativity, in understanding the whole of history, in relationships with other people, and in seeing something of the tremendous scope of the universe from the viewpoint that God exists, God is the Creator, and that He has made us with the capacities we have in His image, to think and act and feel and create on a finite level. As our children are being educated, they are being taught to think and act and feel and to be creative—and we need very much, as parents, to be aware of what is taking place, as much as we are able. To simply assume that school is an education is rather naive in this day and age, it seems to me. Real education can be given in school, and is in some schools, but can also be twisted so that it prevents and 'turns off' any curiosity in the basic areas of the search for real knowledge. To assume that we send our children off to school, and that is it, is shirking the responsibility of being in control, which no one else is going to take, and which God has handed directly to us as Christian parents.[6]

When thinking of the family, we recall the third verse of Psalm 127: "Behold, children are a heritage from the Lord, The fruit of

---

6. Edith Schaeffer, *What is a Family?* (Old Tappan, NJ: Fleming H. Revell, 1975), pp. 170, 171

the womb is His reward." We must not forget, however, that the fourth and fifth verses go on to say that these children are as arrows in the hand of a mighty man, and will speak with the enemies in the gates. In other words, the faith, the values, and the commitments of the parents become the faith, values, and commitments of the children, and they are able to oppose those who would subvert this faith.

The teaching family might not be extinct, but it could be close to qualifying for the endangered species list. The teaching family leaves a legacy for following generations. Any attempt to rebuild society must begin in the Christian home. Strong homes build strong churches and schools!

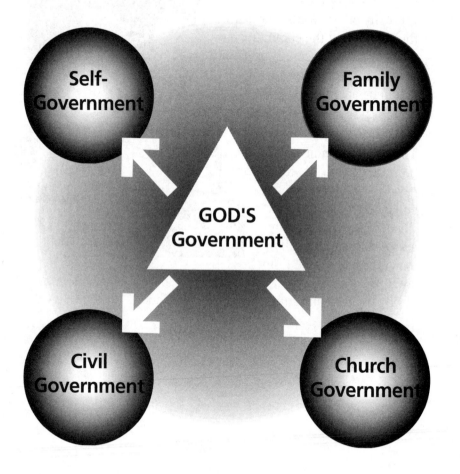

Parental Rights and Responsibilities

Scriptural Authority

In His infinite wisdom, God has instituted four governmental institutions for man in this world: the state, the visible church, the family, and the individual. He has ordained that these four are to coordinate in rights and functions with a mutual interdependence, yet the state, for example, has no more right to usurp the parental sphere than parents do to usurp the state sphere. These coordinate rights and responsibilities, which God has given to each sphere, have been clearly marked out in His Holy Word. This is especially true with respect to the education of children of Christian parents, in defense of which we show forth the following Scripture truths:

1. God instituted the family before either the church or state had existence. Prior to man's fall into sin, the family exercised *total* responsibility over all aspects of God's creation (Genesis 1:27, 28; 2:15–25).

2. God has ordained marriage for the purpose of raising a godly seed through the home and the family institution (Malachi 2:15).

3. The divine legislation given to Moses commands not the state or the church, but the fathers to see to the instruction of the children, that there might be faith and true knowledge in the race to come (Deuteronomy 6:4–7, Psalm 78:3–8).

4. The inspired apostles hold the father directly responsible for consistently bringing up their children in the training and admonition of the Lord (Ephesians 6:4).

5. When children are consecrated to God, the Scriptures call upon the parents to bind themselves by vows before God and man to the faithful discharge of this duty by divine grace (Genesis 17:7–9, 18:19).

6. The blessing of God upon a household is contingent upon the faithful exercise of this parental responsibility, as is so clearly indicated in the case of Abraham and others (Genesis 18:19).

7. The Scriptures clearly state that failure to properly discharge this parental duty immediately disqualifies a man (i.e. the father) from the office of elder in the church (I Timothy 3:4–5, Titus 1:6).

8. In sacred history as recorded in the Scriptures, fathers such as Eli were condemned for their failure to instruct and discipline their children, thus bringing God's judgment on themselves and their house (I Samuel 3:11–14; II Samuel 11:1–27, 12:10–11, 13:1–39, 14:21–33, 15:1–37).

9. Christ, the only sovereign and true Head of the church, who instituted civil government and founded and ordered His Church, has nowhere commanded the state to assume this function, and the state has no authority, as a divinely ordained institution under God and limited by His revealed will, to assume and usurp this responsibility (Deuteronomy 4:2).

10. The state, as a minister of God, is charged with the enforcement of the moral law in human relations, as a temporal ministry of justice among men, and is to protect the family and the church in the free exercise of all their God-given rights and responsibilities (Romans 13:1–10, I Peter 2:13–17, I Timothy 2:1–2).

Therefore, we believe, confess, and maintain that God has committed to parents the high privilege and solemn responsibility of training and educating their children in the fear of the Lord. We further believe that they dare not surrender this God-given right to any other institution, such as the state.

Summary

Education is religious, the Scriptures are the ultimate authority, and parents are accountable to God for the instruction and discipline of their children. Therefore, we cannot in good conscience come under the control of secular authorities with respect to the education of our children.

As God-fearing, law-abiding citizens in full submission to the just and lawful authority of the civil magistrate, we are fully committed to the apostolic precept: "[S]ubmit yourselves to every ordinance of man for the Lord's sake ..." (I Peter 2:13–17, Romans 13:1–7).

If there should be a conflict between the explicit requirements of the Scriptures and the commands of the civil magistrate (an irreconcilable difference between the claims of Christ and of Caesar, which may God in His mercy forbid), we must consistently hold to the superior authority of God speaking through the Scriptures and adhere to that other apostolic precept that we ought "to obey God rather than men" (Acts 5:29).

Worship
in the Home

by Byron Snapp

Training in Godliness the Children of Abraham in the Covenant of Grace

> It needs more than ever to be stressed that the best and truest educators are parents under God. The greatest school is the family. In learning, no act of teaching in any school or university compares to the routine task of mothers in teaching the babe who speaks no language the mother tongue in so short a time. No other task in education is equal to this. The moral training of the child, the discipline of good habits, is an inheritance from parents to the child which surpasses all other. The family is the first and basic school of man.[6]

Parents have the primary responsibility of educating their children. How is this to be carried out? Faithful church attendance and Christian school enrollment are important. Yet, this is not enough. This article will explore an avenue of family instruction that is needed today—that of daily family devotions.

In Psalm 78:4 we read, "We will not hide them from their children, telling to the generation to come the praises of the LORD, and His strength and His wonderful works that He has done." The Hebrew word translated as "hide" here is also used in Isaiah 3:9 … "The look on their countenance witnesses against them, and they declare their sin as Sodom; they do not hide it." This Hebrew phrase, translated "not hide," has the idea of bringing out into the open or declaring openly. Christian parents and heads of households are to declare openly to family members God's law,

---

6. R. J. Rushdoony, *Institutes of Biblical Law* (Phillipsburg, NJ: The Presbyterian and Reformed Publishing Company, 1973), p. 185.

Christ's righteousness, and God's mighty acts. The Psalmist points out the personal responsibility that parents have to faithfully teach their children God's Word. Each generation will do it knowing that God's Word will not return unto Him void, but will accomplish the purpose for which it is sent (Isaiah 55:11).

Although Abraham was approximately one hundred years old, God planned and knew that Abraham would be faithful to teach his household the way of the Lord (Genesis 18:19). The same remains true today. In Ephesians 6:4, Paul commands fathers as follows: "And you fathers, do not provoke your children to wrath, but bring them up in the training and admonition of the Lord." It is quite possible that parents, who neglect to bring up their children according to the Bible, will be angrily blamed when their children see that they are ill-prepared to face their responsibilities with a biblical world and life view. Why would God put this responsibility on parents?

First, our children are to be presented with the mighty acts of God, including the work of the Trinity in regard to salvation and also showing the Lordship of Christ in all of life. God told Abraham of the impending destruction of Sodom and Gomorrah in order that he, his children, and future generations would be reminded of God's mighty act of judgment upon the cities of Sodom and Gomorrah. Our families need to be confronted with the character of our God as He has revealed Himself in Exodus 34:6, 7: "And the LORD passed before him and proclaimed, 'The LORD, the LORD God, merciful and gracious, longsuffering, and abounding in goodness and truth, keeping mercy for thousands, forgiving iniquity and transgression and sin, by no means clearing the guilty, visiting the iniquity of the fathers upon the children and the children's children to the third and the fourth generation.'" In Psalm 78:7, the psalmist aptly sums up the reason for instructing present and future generations: "That they may set their hope in God, And not forget the works of God, But keep His commandments."

A daily period of family worship is certainly part of the diligent instruction mentioned in Deuteronomy 6:7.

Some calculation might underscore this importance. Assuming you attend church once a week, over a fifteen-year period you have attended church 780 times. If you have daily devotions over the same period, you will have been able to lead your family in the study of Scripture and worship of God 5,478 times. In a fifty-year period, that would be 18,262 occasions of worship in the home—taking into account leap years.

Is your church, or body of elders, stressing this family responsibility? In his book, *Thoughts on Family Worship*, James W. Alexander speaks of past days in which presbyteries would visit churches within their bounds.

> By the Act of Assembly, 1596, ratified December 17, 18, 1638, among other provisions for the visitation of churches by presbyteries, the following questions were proposed to the heads of families: "Do the elders visit the families within the quarter and bounds assigned to each of them? Are they careful to have the worship of God set up in the families of their bounds?"[7]

---

7. B. M. Palmer and James W. Alexander, *The Family* (Harrisonburg, VA: Sprinkle Publications, 1991)—two books in one volume; this quote is taken from the second book, written by J. W. Alexander, entitled *Thoughts on Family Worship*, p. 24.

If you are an elder, I ask you, are you in your visitation checking into family worship among your church membership? I ask each reader, are you seeking to instruct this generation and future generations in your home concerning the Word of God? Parents of baptized children need to be reminded periodically that they have promised to pray with and for their children and to teach their children biblical doctrine.

Secondly, parents are reminded by conducting family worship, that throughout the day they are setting the law of God before family members in their words and actions (Deuteronomy 6:4–9). Family worship reminds all members that their dependence is upon God for all things day and night. In their daily steps, God's Word is to be a lamp to their feet and a light to their path (Psalm 119:105). Parents realize as their household submits itself to the instruction of Scripture during devotions, that some submission must extend throughout the day. It is hard for a parent to sit down and conduct family worship if he does not, throughout the day, seek to practice, by God's grace, what he teaches.

Family devotions provide an opportunity for the father to instruct his household to look at all of life through God's spectacles—the Bible. The Book of Proverbs provides many illustrations of this. The father is careful to point out to his son, as he prepares to go into the world, that godly wisdom must be the basis for all his decisions (Proverbs 1:7, 2:1–4, 4:1–9). Children will be more apt to teach their children daily if they themselves have been taught by their parents.

No one can be saved because of the merits of family worship. Salvation comes only when one is convicted by the Holy Spirit of his sin, and flees to Christ in faith and repentance. Yet, family worship provides further opportunities for the unregenerate in your home to hear the Gospel. It provides the opportunity for overnight guests also to be confronted with the truths of Scripture.

Many readers say that this sounds good, but for one reason or another this could not be put into practice in their home.

Some might feel they are too old to begin family worship. Abraham had seen his ninety-ninth birthday (Genesis 17:1) when

God stated in Genesis 18:19 that Abraham would command his children and his household after him to keep God's Word. The fact is, as long as God leaves us here, we are to instruct those around us in the things of God. We are never too old. Redeem the time that remains for you upon the earth by instructing those in your household in the way of the Lord. After his encounter with the man at Peniel, Jacob was commanded in Genesis 35:1 to go to Bethel, to live and worship God. Notice that Jacob tells his household in verse 2: "And Jacob said to his household and to all who were with him, 'Put away the foreign gods that are among you, purify yourselves, and change your garments.'" The point I want to make here is that Jacob saw error in his household. As head of his household, he commanded that it be corrected according to God's standards. We, as heads of household, never become too old nor lose the God-given responsibility to correct error in our homes.

Some readers may say they are too few in number. The children are grown and gone. Perhaps only you and your wife remain. Perhaps you have just married. You say that you will begin family devotions when God gives you children. In Matthew 18:20 we read: "For where two or three are gathered together in My name, I am there in the midst of them."

Christ promises to be with His people, no matter how small in number, when they meet in worship. Family worship is not just for children, it is for the family. Husbands and wives need this daily time before God's Word as well. Continued Bible reading, discussion, and prayer on a daily basis is important for whoever may be in your household, before you have children or after they have married and left.

Another often-heard excuse is, "We're too busy. Both parents work. The children are involved in extra-curricular activities, etc." Christ once heard a similar complaint. It is recorded in Luke 10:38–40. Martha, busy cooking a meal for Jesus, becomes extremely upset with her sister Mary. Mary was sitting at the feet of Jesus drinking in His every Word. Martha asks Jesus to rebuke Mary for not helping her. Instead, Jesus admonishes Martha, "Martha, Martha, you are worried and troubled about many things. But one thing is needed, and Mary has chosen that good part, which will not be taken away from her" (Luke 10:41,42). Jesus was not stating that all we need to do is read the Bible, not worrying about building His Kingdom. He is stating that Christians are not to become so involved in their pursuits and obligations that they neglect to feed upon the law of God. You find time to eat every day. You find time to enjoy your favorite television program. Are these more important than family worship? It is important that you make time for that which is most important.

A lack of family devotions must be based on excuses only, for no acceptable reasons can be found to support their absence. As Christians, we look forward to our children being better Christians than we are. We long to see society further reconstructed for God's glory in their generation. Part of our present obligation is to faithfully teach God's Word to our household. Are family devotions a part of your daily life?

Recently, the fire alarm in an Indiana fire station rang. The firemen immediately responded to the call. In their haste, they forgot to turn off their own stove. The alarm was false. Upon returning to their station, they found it in flames. Much damage was done before the flames were extinguished. I believe this illustrates the situation existing in the homes of many Christians today.

Many are busy answering alarms that later in life will be seen as of little importance compared with the need for daily biblical instruction in the home. We want our families to be involved in recreational activities, cultural opportunities, etc., which are important. Yet, unintentionally, these in addition to television, newspapers, etc., crowd out daily family devotions.

In this article, we want to examine benefits derived from family devotions and list some practical helps for these times of worship.

One benefit of family devotions is that a specific daily opportunity is given to further equip household members to stand against and battle humanism. In Psalm 78:1–6 the Psalmist speaks of the need to teach God's law to each generation. A reason for so doing is given in verse 7: "That they may set their hope in God, and not forget the works of God, but keep His commandments."

In verses 9–11 of this Psalm, mention is made of the children of Ephraim who, being armed, "turned back in the day of battle." They refused to walk according to God's law. They forgot His mighty works. They had the weapons and the opportunity to drive out the godless from the land God gave them. They failed. They turned back in the day of battle. Any generation that has not been faithfully taught God's Word will react in the same manner. A similar situation had happened years earlier in Israel's history, after the death of Joshua's generation. In Judges 2:10 we read, "when all that generation had been gathered to their fathers, another generation arose after them who did not know the LORD nor the work which He had done for Israel." Their parents had been busy in conquering and settling the land. Evidently, many felt biblical instruction ought to be left for others. In his unpublished work, *Ancient Israel's War Against Humanism—A Practical Commentary on the Book of Judges* (Part One: Judges 1–12), James B. Jordan makes the following important comments:

> Israel's national disasters were a direct result of the family disasters, parents who did not understand God's priorities. Busy-busy Christians and their rebellious children: a story

common to all ages of the Church. And is this not why so many preachers' kids and missionaries' kids turn out bad?

And how often is this simply the result of parental egotism? I'm important and my work is important, and I don't have time for my children. Parents with such attitudes will pay dearly in their old age, and so will society [p.20].

Many Christians today are making the same mistake as did the children of Ephraim. The next generation is being sent into the battle against humanism with their weapon, God's Word (Ephesians 6:17), readily accessible. They flee from battle with their weapon unused because they are ignorant of the mighty works of God. Knowing not the Lord, they naturally openly express their allegiance to humanism. Often Scripture is wrongly used to back up their claims.

Israel repeatedly failed as a nation because parents failed to faithfully teach their children the Word of God. Our nation stands on the brink of great judgment today. How many of your children know that the basic battle in society today is that of Christianity vs. Humanism? How many have seen from daily instruction that Scripture alone speaks to personal, family, and civil problems? Do you desire to have your family pray with the Psalmist: "Let my heart be blameless regarding your statutes, that I may not be ashamed" (Psalm 119:80)? Salvation is by God's grace alone. He alone can give faith and repentance. It cannot be stressed too much that our families need diligent, daily instruction in God's Word, accompanied by prayer; that God will use it for the furtherance of His Kingdom.

Secondly, family devotions give the opportunity for greater unity within the family. Christian families are not perfect. There will be husband-wife disputes and sibling quarrels. How are disagreements to be handled? Paul teaches in Ephesians 4:26 that we are not to let the sun set on our anger. The time to deal with anger is the moment it occurs. Because of our own pride, we do not want to be reconciled in the heat of anger. Have you tried to sincerely pray with someone with whom you were mad? I do not believe it can be done. Reconciliation must first take place (Matthew 5:23,24). As families gather daily to worship God, bitterness among family members must be resolved or else the time will only be a ceremony worthy of God's anger. The husband and wife must have disagreements settled. They must be ready to ask for God's will to be done.

Family problems cannot be swept under the rug and given the opportunity to incubate and hatch into a bigger problem.

The old slogan "The family that prays together stays together," contains much truth. Prayer is not something that allows a couple to live an antinomian lifestyle and pray once a day in the assurance of a solid marriage. The family that truly prays together can only do so after differences are resolved. Frequently, God will use the two-edged sword of His Word to cut away at the anger and bring conviction and repentance as the family members submit themselves to the authority of Scripture.

A third benefit of devotions is that of practical instruction as to how to read and study Scripture and how to pray. As children hear Dad and Mom pray and join in vocal prayers themselves, their prayer lives will be strengthened. Children will be encouraged to pray in Christian schools, in church, in college dorms, and in their future families, having had this background. Greater opportunity is also given for becoming more familiar with psalms and hymns as they are sung during this time.

Practical Guidelines for Family Devotions

Psalm 78:4 reminds us that we are to teach future generations. Let us now consider some practical guidelines for conducting family devotions.

We must remember that we want to conduct *family* devotions. All inhabitants of our household should be present. It is the responsibility of the father and the mother to arrange schedules accordingly.

> *And Jesus answered and said to her, "Martha, Martha, you are worried and troubled about many things. But one thing is needed, and Mary has chosen that good part, which will not be taken away from her."*
>
> *Luke 10:41, 42*

This may require everyone getting up a few minutes earlier each morning. The situation will be different for each family. Each family will be tempted to say their schedule cannot be rearranged. Let us not forget our covenantal responsibilities to teach and pray with our families. Memorize Luke 10:41, 42: "And Jesus answered and said to her, 'Martha, Martha, you are worried and troubled about many things. But one thing is needed, and Mary has chosen that good part, which will not be taken away from her.'" Hide these words in your heart that they might remind you to arrange your schedule in such a way that your family can be instructed daily.

We need to also find a time when there will be the least interruption. The phone may need to be taken off the hook. If relatives or friends are in a habit of dropping by during this time, invite them to stay or inform them in love that you have set aside this time for Bible study. Invite them to come at another time.

Try to schedule your devotional time when your family is as alert as possible. They should not be held at a time when you have to rush through them because everyone's mind is on their upcoming favorite television show.... Don't prolong the time, but allow for an adequate time together.

Devotions must not become a ritual or a formality. The desire is for family members to incline their ear to wisdom and their heart to understanding (Proverbs 2:2). Variation helps to promote this, humanly speaking. From personal experience, we have found it best to begin our time with prayer, realizing that God's Spirit must give us fertile hearts and minds for His Word. Scripture then is read and discussed. Although a multitude of devotional books are available, they must not take the place of the Bible. Care must be taken that we do not just read man's comments upon a text without reading Scripture itself. The Bible must always be pre-eminent. We have found it helpful to discuss the passage among all family members. I stress this because it is easy to have the false idea that the Bible study is only for children; they must be asked all the questions. Every family member should be asked a question and should be encouraged to enter into the discussion. Knowing that questions will be asked will help some members to keep alert while the passage is being read. At times you may want to sing one or two psalms or hymns. Also, you may show a picture of a missionary family, relate something about their work and pray for them. Catechism questions can be reviewed occasionally.[8] You can think of other variations.

In closing, a couple of warnings must be given. Let no parent think that this is the only time he needs to speak to his children about the Lord. Deuteronomy 6:4–9 is very clear. Parents are to faithfully teach Scripture in word, deed, and action. We always have the responsibility to reconstruct family life and society by the faithful application of God's Word.

Scripture reminds us that to whom much is given, much is required (Luke 12:48). Faithful family devotions must result in an attitude of humility, not pride. We must not think ourselves better than others who are perhaps weaker in the faith. Greater study of God's Word, by His grace, results in greater knowledge

---

8. The following catechisms are recommended for families to use: (1) the Heidelberg Catechism or the Westminster Shorter Catechism, for older children, and (2) the *First Catechism* or *A Catechism for Boys and Girls*, for younger children. Vic Lockman has also created *The Westminster Shorter Catechism with Cartoons* for children of all ages. These catechisms cover all the main doctrines of Scripture.

which, in turn, results in greater responsibility to apply the crown rights of Christ throughout life.

As you begin this, and continue it, your family will be tempted to give up. As your children mature, schedules will have to be continually rearranged. From time to time there will be new types of interruptions. Some days you will fail to have this time together. Endeavor anew after these failures to reclaim this time with your family in order that your household might better "set their hope in God, and not forget the works of God, but keep His commandments" (Psalm 78:7).

Discipline

by Dr. Paul Lindstrom

Making Disciples

To discipline children means to make them disciples, to drill and educate them, and to bring them into effective obedience to a person or a cause. To chastise children is to rebuke them in some fashion for behavior unbecoming a disciple. Chastisement is corrective and merciful in purpose (Hebrews 12:5–11). Chastening is evidence of a father's love and concern that his children become faithful disciples.

Chastisement without discipline is ineffective. Too many parents think that by beating their children or scolding them endlessly, they will thereby discipline them effectively. Unless someone is first of all disciplined—made an obedient follower—chastisement accomplishes nothing. All that remains for that person is punishment and judgment (Proverbs 22:6).

Christian discipline is instruction and guidance into an orderly way of life which becomes second nature to the disciple. The child is systematically trained in the faith, in knowledge of the Bible and its requirements, and in every necessary area of study, so that it becomes a part of his nature. He acts and reacts in terms of this training. In other words, his thoughts, words, and actions are Christ-like.

Christian discipline is a necessary part of sanctification. Basic to discipline is regeneration. It is the regenerate man who is best disciplined, because he has the foundation—a new nature—which is in full harmony with the discipline required of him. The more he grows in terms of that discipline, the more useful he becomes to his Lord.

Discipline is the process of being *educated* by God, wherever we are. The purpose of education is to fit children to be servants of God; discipline is education of children for God.

Believing that chastening is necessary for the welfare of the student as well as the entire school, we would suggest the following Christian principles and guidelines as set forth in the Scriptures. Read Proverbs 3:11–12; 13:24; 29:15–17.

The Teacher as Student

Learning involves *discipline, motivation,* and *communication.*

1. **Discipline:** Learning is in part a discipline. An undisciplined teacher is usually a poor learner and a poor teacher. What are the marks of an undisciplined person? He has a growing backlog of work which never gets done. He has difficulty getting started with a task, so necessary tasks remain undone. Duties become unpleasant because he is increasingly beset with guilt over all the unfinished duties. Anxiety and lack of rest result.

   Our problem is this: the work we least like to do, we postpone until last, and then, being tired, we have all kinds of good excuses for not doing it. We fool ourselves into thinking that, if we can start by doing a few things we like, we will be off and running—able to tackle everything. In theory this sounds good. In practice human nature does not operate this way. The key to a successful work discipline is to do all those things we least like to do first. We do them with a fresher mind. Having done them, we free ourselves to do those things we enjoy doing. Instead of working with a nagging sense of guilt, we work with a happy freedom. Moreover, we work with greater efficiency, effectiveness, and a clearer mind.

   Our teaching must be well organized and systematic. If we ourselves are not prone to being orderly in our thinking, our teaching will not be so. Therefore, the superior teacher is always disciplining himself in order to pass on disciplined learning to his pupils.

2. **Motivation:** We cannot give others a desire to learn if we do not have it. Most good teachers enjoy studying. A teacher can teach pupils how to read, but a love of reading comes, in part, from a teacher who shares that love. To motivate our students, we too must be motivated.

3. **Communication:** The teacher who does not grow in his knowledge of his subject, in methodology and content, is a very limited teacher, and his pupils are *under-privileged* learners.

   In all teaching we communicate with our pupils. One of the dangers of being a teacher is that we are always talking. By allowing the student to talk and express himself, we often receive very valuable insights into his thinking, which enables us to realistically communicate.

Summary

The teacher as student is, above all else, a student of God's Word. To be a student means to advance and grow. To our children we are teachers. It is a good example and inspiration to our children that they see their parents studying and growing in knowledge.

Accountability and Structure

by Michael J. McHugh[9]

God is glorified when His people adopt structured approaches to education simply because such approaches are consistent with how God Himself operates. The sovereign Lord of Scripture and Creation is, after all, a God of order and not a God of confusion. In the book of First Corinthians, chapter 14, we read, "Let all things be done decently and in order" (verse 40). Therefore, more parents need to ask themselves, "Does our approach to home education reflect this biblical standard?"

It is imperative that Christian home educators reject educational methods that put a child's interest in being entertained ahead of his need to learn with continuity and accountability. As the Bible states in Lamentations 3:27, "It is good for a man to bear the yoke in his youth." It needs to be stressed at the outset, that the way God has ordained for children to obtain the *crown* of a truly excellent education is through the *cross* of disciplined study—our children must be lovingly trained to see that the way to the crown is the way of the cross. Children need to know that the learning process is often difficult and wearisome, but in spite of the difficulties, is still what God's children are called to pursue.

True education, from a biblical perspective, is not a random pursuit of learning without clearly defined goals. Rather, it is a structured line-upon-line, precept upon precept, exercise that has clear academic and spiritual goals in view (see the example given in Deuteronomy 6:4–9).

---

9. Michael McHugh has labored in the field of Christian home education with the CLASS program for over twenty years. During his time with the CLASS ministry, he has worked as a teacher, curriculum director, and textbook author. He and his wife have been involved in homeschooling their six children for over a decade.

This is not to say, of course, that the learning process should leave no room for creativity or spontaneous exploration. Such unplanned pursuits have their place. However, it is only when educators have taken the time to clearly define their goals that they can afford to safely venture off

their main trail of learning for brief periods. In other words, you cannot find your way back to your goals effectively unless you had a clear path set forth in the first place.

In a similar respect, true teaching, biblically speaking, is preoccupied with the process of making disciples. Discipleship, however, assumes that there is someone who is leading and someone who is following the leader. Any Christian teacher, therefore, who desires to instruct a child must first have that student under control. Sadly, many Christian home educators today are failing to recognize that the utilization of a disciplined approach to homeschooling is a prerequisite for producing disciples—no consistent discipline, no disciples. Moreover, if we are not interested in producing graduates that are disciples of Christ, then why are we in the education business?

The staff of the Christian Liberty Academy School System (CLASS) firmly believes that discipleship is at the heart of the learning process in home teaching. We also believe that it is counterproductive to approach the vital task of training disciples in an unstructured manner. For this reason, CLASS rejects the popular notion that learning must be child-directed and entertaining in its presentation.

So many magazine ads and promotional materials—written to influence the home school community in the twenty-first century—stress that homeschooling can and should be easy and fun. Quite frankly, this propaganda sounds too good to be true for the simple reason that it is! Families who enroll their children in the CLASS home school program quickly realize that our focus is not fun and games. We are serious about exposing young people to a rigorous and thorough course of study that is carefully planned and structured to prepare children to enter the harsh and demanding world of college or career.

Although CLASS families are given a meaningful degree of flexibility over how they pursue their children's training, and are encouraged to pursue supplemental activities with their students—the basic core subjects are clearly laid out in a logical sequence. The CLASS course of study seldom, if ever, asks the student to set his or her own agenda. Rather, the assumption is that young minds need to be guided into the truth in an orderly manner. In the perspective of the CLASS faculty, any home school that permits or encourages students to set their own academic or spiritual goals, apart from the input of knowledgeable parents or mature educators, is making a serious mistake.

It is ironic to see how many parents within the home school community, who would never think of permitting their children to determine their own wardrobe or mode of dress, turn around and permit the same children to choose what type of curriculum they wish to use. In spite of the fact that the Bible clearly teaches that foolishness is bound up in the heart of a child, some Christian parents still feel persuaded to let the so-called "natural love of learning"—that each child is assumed to possess—take charge over the learning agenda.

Now it should be granted that, if young students were truly angels who by nature were self-motivated, sinless, inherently mature, and self-disciplined, then structured home school programs with accountability would be quite unnecessary. But as a Christian dad with six homeschooled children and over twenty years of professional experience in working with literally thousands of home schoolers across the world, I can assure you that even Christian students are not angels. As the Book of Proverbs states so plainly in chapter 29:15, "The rod and reproof give wisdom, but a child left to himself brings shame to his mother."

Far too many home schoolers crash and burn in their efforts to educate their children because they assume that they can do without a structured approach to their children's education.

Another assumption that frequently undermines the success of home education is the belief that every parent is well-suited to home school without outside support or accountability. While it is certainly true that some parents are well-suited to home school on an independent basis, my own experiences in the homeschooling movement have taught me that many are not best served by approaching home education as the lone ranger.

For over twenty years, the staff at Christian Liberty has observed thousands of parents, who have embarked upon the path of independence, fall victim to what may be called the "Red October Syndrome." Every October, without fail, we are contacted by parents who began their school year on an independent basis and soon realized that they were not prospering. Many more, however, begin to flounder in October and give up a short time later, without ever contacting our school. In my perspective, the home school community has been receiving a rather one-sided and artificially rosy picture of independent homeschooling for many years. As one who frequently attends home school conventions and book fairs across the country, I have never noted one person to be given the opportunity to explain why they failed in their experiment of independent home education. On the other hand, I have heard numerous convention speakers extol the virtues of homeschooling without outside support or accountability.

Seldom, if ever, are parents given any warnings about the pitfalls of independent home education.

I firmly believe that any parents who are seriously considering an independent approach to home schooling should begin by asking themselves several practical questions:

First: Do I, by nature, tend to take the easy way around teaching academic material that is extra challenging?

Second: Am I a self-starter who needs little outside accountability to stay on schedule and meet deadlines?

Third: Do I, as a teacher, tolerate mediocre performance when my student expresses frustration?

Fourth: Can I objectively evaluate my own children's progress or do I tend to be too easy or too hard on my children?

Fifth: Am I skilled at not only buying curriculum materials but also planning course objectives? Can I afford the time to do both jobs well? How do I know that my plan will work at all?

Lastly: In addition to doing all of the equipping, teaching, and evaluating for my children, can I also keep the type of permanent records that will be recognized by colleges?

As I hope each reader will realize, these serious and down-to-earth questions must be dealt with by parents before they set sail on the sea of independent home education. If more parents carefully and prayerfully examined their readiness to home school without outside support, we would see less families running back to public or private schools. Children should not be the objects of experimentation when parents have time-tested, Christ-honoring schools with which they can partner in the awesome task of training their children for Christ.

As a home school dad, I know firsthand how easy it is for home school parents who are caught up in the busyness of life to unintentionally let things slide. I cannot help but believe that some of you who are reading this message can relate to this fact as well. Although it is humbling, and even slightly embarrassing, more parents who are already committed to homeschooling with accountability need to admit that they need the help of other educators within the body of Christ. It is my sincere belief that God will bless those who have the humility to admit that they cannot do a difficult task without the help of others. Pride indeed does come before a fall, and the primary purpose of this message is to keep families from falling victim to the assumption that they can do it all, even before they carefully examine their own qualifications.

When parents enter the deep waters of home education, they should remember the rule that every scuba diver learns—never dive alone. This concept is known as the "buddy system." More home educators should ask themselves: "Who is my buddy?"

Building of a Successful Home School

There are, obviously, many facets to the building of a successful home school; just as an architect sits down to plan out the details of a home he is designing, home school parents must be sure to build wisely and with structural integrity. Let's consider for several moments the analogy of building a home and relate that to the building of a successful home school.

The first step in designing any structure is to put together a master plan; such plans are often known as blueprints. In the case of home schoolers, it is their curriculum goals—which are informed by their philosophy or worldview—that are their blueprints. All home educators should commit themselves to working within an educational framework that has comprehensive goals established for each student's academic, physical, and spiritual life. Buying a pile of books, that merely seeks to address the ever changing interests of students, is not the same as designing a curriculum to fit into a master plan.

The actual building process begins with the foundation. For home schoolers to erect a stable and enduring educational structure, it is vital that they build upon a solid foundation. The only true foundation for education and life is the truth of God's Word. The bricks that help to make your structure are your books or educational materials. When selecting resources or curriculum materials, home educators must insist upon a Christ-centered orientation to the materials. Such parents must be discerning enough to look beyond fancy packaging and electronic gadgetry to analyze whether curriculum materials are consistent with the standards of Holy Scripture.

Every home also needs some kind of roof to protect it from the harsh elements of sin that can damage the learning process and harm the parent-child relationship. For the Christian home schooler, prayer is the instrument that must be used to protect the home from the elements of sin and its destructive influences. Parent teachers must pray with and for their students daily.

The building of any home would not be complete without windows and a door. Windows are put in a home so that the occupants can have the pleasure of looking outside on the world around them. When parents look through the windows of their home, they should remind themselves that they have a duty to prepare their children to overcome the world. Only a disciplined commitment to excellence will ensure that a child is ready to face the outside world. For better or for worse, parents are only given

Structure for Home Education

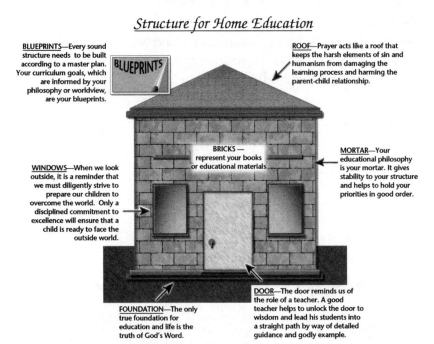

BLUEPRINTS—Every sound structure needs to be built according to a master plan. Your curriculum goals, which are informed by your philosophy or worldview, are your blueprints.

ROOF—Prayer acts like a roof that keeps the harsh elements of sin and humanism from damaging the learning process and harming the parent-child relationship.

WINDOWS—When we look outside, it is a reminder that we must diligently strive to prepare our children to overcome the world. Only a disciplined commitment to excellence will ensure that a child is ready to face the outside world.

BRICKS — represent your books or educational materials

MORTAR—Your educational philosophy is your mortar. It gives stability to your structure and helps to hold your priorities in good order.

FOUNDATION—The only true foundation for education and life is the truth of God's Word.

DOOR—The door reminds us of the role of a teacher. A good teacher helps to unlock the door to wisdom and lead his students into a straight path by way of detailed guidance and godly example.

one opportunity to prepare their students well. No home would be complete without a door. The door reminds us of the role of the teacher. A good teacher helps to unlock the door to wisdom and lead his students into a straight path by way of detailed guidance and godly example. No amount of video tapes or computers can ever replace the vital human interaction that must take place between teacher and students. The ultimate example of a true DOOR is the Master Teacher Jesus Christ. The Lord Jesus is the best model to follow, for He knew how to lead people to wisdom and how to make disciples.

The goal of Christian home education must consistently be that of training disciples who will be soldiers in Christ's Kingdom. The world your children will enter is a battleground, not a playground. At CLASS, we are serious about partnering with parents to raise a generation of men and women who can turn the world upside down for the glory of King Jesus.

In closing, I would like to encourage families to do all things decently and in order—including the task of home education. Your children deserve to be trained within an educational system that provides parental nurturing and academic excellence that is based upon proven results.

As you look to the future, we trust that God will continue to give you wisdom and discernment in regard to the ideal manner in which to teach your children.

Helping Children Learn Better

by Richard Best

Parents and educators, consider the following questions:

Do you feel your children should be doing better in school? Do your children have trouble motivating themselves to work hard consistently? Do your children appear to be working hard but don't have as much to show for their efforts as they deserve?

If you answer "Yes" to any or all of these questions, I am confident that you will find this article useful.

What can you do to help your children learn better?

Before trying to suggest some answers, we should first examine two primary reasons why many students are not learning and performing as well as they could.

1. Many students do not learn well and do not seem interested in school because they don't spend time learning. For these children, school assignments are often in sharp contrast to their non-school activities; they are not used to the type of thinking required of them in school. A primary reason why students find reading boring is because they do very little of it unless they have to. Many of our students approach school in a passive way, acting as observers and not as participants in their learning.

2. A second factor limiting performance is not that students cannot learn well, but that many do not know **how** to learn well. They have not mastered the tools necessary to be successful learners. This skill deficiency limits the capacity for success and, in doing so, often limits the motivation potential. It results in students finding school to be a frustrating and discouraging experience.

These two factors provide important insights for developing strategies to enhance your children's learning. They also point out inadequacies in telling students:

"You simply have to work harder."

"You have to get interested in the subject."

While encouraging children to work harder carries some merit, there are limits to its usefulness. What do you do with children who have become discouraged and frustrated with schoolwork? It's hard for such students to make the effort when they have so little to show for it. Moreover, what do you do if your children are already working hard but just not succeeding? Finally, how can you expect students to get interested in or motivated for a subject, if they do not know how to study the subject well?

If "working harder" and "getting more interested" are not sure-fire solutions, how can you help your children learn better?

One important answer lies in helping them to become more able and confident in the process of learning, to assist them in developing key learning skills in learning how to learn. Knowing how to learn results in better performance and this improved performance leads to increased motivation. The following diagram conveys the importance of skills:

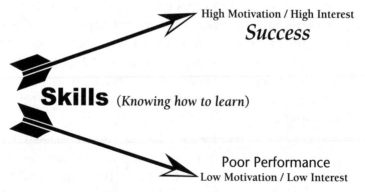

If developing these learning skills is so important, you are likely to ask: "What are these skills? What can I do to help my children master them?"

Following are six key principles which are especially important for success in school.

Principle 1:
Using an Effective Approach

What often limits students' performance is not a lack of ability but a lack of an effective approach. Unfortunately, the two become confused by teachers, parents, and students themselves.

Reading provides a vivid illustration of this. How do you think most students approach reading assignments? Typically they will:

1. Open to the assignment with the primary goal of finishing it.
2. Start at the beginning of the assignment with little sense as to what the passage is about.
3. Move from paragraph to paragraph without pausing to think about the material.
4. Close the book immediately after completing the last word and move on to something else.

What happens if your children read like this? In most cases they will have little to show for their efforts; words and ideas go in and come right back out. This negative experience reinforces the attitude that reading is unrewarding, boring, and frustrating. Finally, this approach increases the likelihood that they will read ineffectively the next time. Thus the cycle continues.

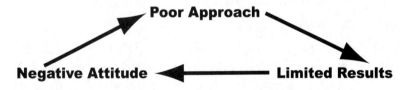

What are the ingredients for effective reading?

1. Preview the assignment first. Have some idea of what the passage is about before beginning to read.
2. Make up questions from section headings (if textbook) before reading each section. This provides a focus, a purpose for reading.

3. Pause periodically to think about the material. Try to summarize the key ideas in your own words. Try to answer the questions.

4. Underline key points. Take notes without merely copying the author's words.

5. Review important points upon completing the assignment.

What happens if your children read in this manner? Such an approach increases the quality of the reading experience. It insures that students have something to show for their efforts, and maximizes the chances for reading to be viewed as worthwhile and enjoyable.

This principle of effective approach can be applied to any type of assignment, such as writing a paper, solving word problems, taking a test, listening or taking notes, etc. Whatever the assignment, successful learners figure out what their effective approach is. The more you can assist them in that process, the better chances they will have for a positive learning experience.

Principle 2:
Using a Question-and-Answer Method:
Being an Active Learner

Look back to the two reading methods outlined above. The difference between them is that the first is a **passive** approach while the second is an **active** one. Passive learners simply look at or hear words without really thinking about them. Active students question themselves about the material, try to explain key ideas in their own words. For the passive learner, words "go in one ear and out the other." Active students better understand and remember.

In addition to reading, the idea of active learning—using a question-and-answer approach—applies to other academic skills.

Testing Preparation	Make up likely questions and practice answering them. Practice taking the test before actually having to take it.
Listening	Summarize key points mentally as the teacher is talking. Become involved in class.
Note taking	Write questions in the margin alongside the notes, cover up the answers, look at the questions and try to explain the notes.

Studying in such an active, questioning way insures not only that your children will learn better but learn faster as well.

How can you help your children to use such an approach?

1. Be question facilitators, not answer providers.
2. Encourage them to use these active approaches in their classes.
3. Encourage them to explain ideas. This will help them to understand better what they are studying.

Principle 3:
Creating Clear Relationships Between Ideas

Which of the two pictures below would be easier to understand and remember?

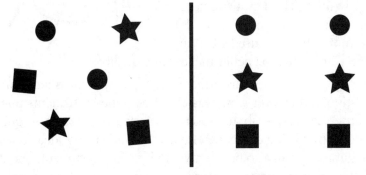

Obviously, the one on the right is easier because it has an order, a logic, and organization; it makes sense. This principle applies to learning ideas as well as the patterns of figures. Students must take the time to see how ideas fit together.

How can students apply this principle to their classes? Outlining and making up summary review sheets from their notes and reading are two ways. Being a question-and-answer student is another; it is an essential sorting out method.

Principle 4:
Selecting Key Ideas

In addition to organizing ideas, it is also necessary to select the key information. Being able to identify what is most important can make learning easier. Why? The brain has limits as to how much it can take in at any one time. Moreover, taking the time to identify the key ideas assists learning as it encourages thinking about the material. Finally, trying to learn everything often results in poor learning.

Encourage your children to summarize what they read, hear, or study.

Principle 5:
Using All Learning Channels

Learning channels refer to different pathways by which information travels to the brain. They include: seeing, hearing, saying and writing. The key to remember about these channels is that the more channels used in trying to learn something, the better the learning quality.

One way of applying this principle is explaining ideas aloud in a question-and-answer way. This could be done by students questioning themselves about reading material, notes, or test questions or by having someone else test them. Writing ideas out in the same way can also be effective. In both cases, students should try to explain in their own words.

Principle 6:
Creating a Productive Learning Environment

What are the characteristics of such an environment? Let us start with three primary ones:

1. Distractions must be minimized.
2. Time must be managed well.
3. Clear goals must be established.

The lack of such ingredients limits the possibilities for successful learning.

Concentration/Minimizing Distractions—Concentration is a key tool for students as it increases learning potential; therefore your children learn better and learn faster if they are not bombarded with considerable distractions. If part of the brain is studying and another part of the brain is trying to watch television or relax on the bed or decide what to do this weekend, learning quality is compromised.

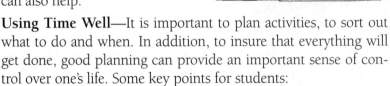

Encourage your children to cut down on noise, especially people talking, TV, or loud music. Studying at a desk or table, a place that is comfortable but not too comfortable, can also help.

Using Time Well—It is important to plan activities, to sort out what to do and when. In addition, to insure that everything will get done, good planning can provide an important sense of control over one's life. Some key points for students:

1. Write out an agenda for the day.
2. Plan both on a daily basis as well as a long-term basis.
3. Get an early start on long-term projects.
4. Set specific and reasonable goals.
5. Get work done as early in the day as possible.

Some Final Remarks

When used, these learning principles are both practical and helpful. However, helping children to use them is much easier said than done. The more they feel that this is something they wish to initiate, the greater the probability that change will occur. Ultimately, they must take responsibility for making these changes.

PART 3

The Form of Christian Homeschooling

The Character of Your Classroom

Conditions for Learning

We have found that students learn most eagerly and effectively:

- when they see the need to approach learning from a Christian perspective;
- when they are given clear, concise instructions, with examples and meaningful practice;
- when they regularly summarize what they have learned;
- when variety is used to hold their interest while covering similar material;
- when they can relate their studies to real life, rather than learn apparently unrelated facts; and
- when they can evaluate their learning and can strive to correct their own mistakes.

Classroom Basics

Follow a Regular Schedule

Choose a regular time and place for teaching sessions and adhere to that schedule each day.

Limit Distractions

Choose a study place as free from distractions as possible. If necessary, switch off the ringer on your phone, and definitely turn off the radio and television. Do all of this for the sake of your student's concentration. Children will enjoy studying much more if they are not distracted.

Be Prepared

Read over lesson material and set out all needed items such as pencils and erasers before beginning class. If you are prepared ahead of time, you will maintain your children's interest much longer.

Be Goal-oriented

Never lose sight of what you are trying to teach in each lesson. It is very easy to get side-tracked and forget both immediate and ultimate purposes. Don't allow your children, some of whom may be adept at derailing their parents, to lead you away from your goals.

Be Interested

Show your children that you are interested in them and in what they do. They, in turn, will want to impress you and will strive to do well. Demonstrate genuine interest in what you teach, as well. Your children are more likely to love the subject you're excited about than the one you tell them they have to "get through." Maintain your own enthusiasm by trying a new approach or tracking down information on a related topic which you or your students find intriguing.

Keep Instruction Low Key

Encourage your children and avoid sarcasm. Make them feel successful no matter how little they seem to learn on any given day. It is necessary to correct mistakes, but children do not usually mind if you do it kindly and constructively. Do not expect perfection; only God is without error.

Give Praise

Few things will encourage children more than praise given by parents for real accomplishment, no matter how small. Every paper graded "100" is as important to a child as a salary increase is to his parents. When an accomplishment of any size occurs, view it through your child's eyes and reward him accordingly.

Make Lessons Reasonable

Avoid tiring your children with lengthy lessons and working beyond their attention spans. Don't expect or require more of your children than they are capable of producing at their age. You don't have to complete every lesson in a single sitting. Quitting a few minutes early now and then will have little effect on how much your child learns. It can make a great difference, however, in how much you and your children enjoy the process.

Take a Break

After a half hour of study with younger children—a bit longer with older students—set studies aside for a few moments. Determine break times in advance and stick to them. There is danger in making a break too long or too short. A break that is too brief will not refresh your child. If the break is too long, the student may break his learning stride. Three to five minutes is adequate. Have the student stretch, walk around, get a bite to eat or drink, talk with the family, and then get back to studying.

Be Alert to Frustration

If a child does not seem to understand the ideas you are presenting, perhaps you should step back for a moment and try to determine the cause. Are you pushing too hard? Have you prepared the child for this material? Does your approach assume too much knowledge, maturity, or skill on the child's part? If you still make no progress after such an adjustment, take a full day off from the troublesome subject. A fresh approach may help the child begin to understand the topic.

Display Achievement

Make up a classroom wall chart (K–6) to show your student's progress. Mark it off in grids vertically and horizontally, showing the days of the month, or the weeks of the month, and the student's subjects in the resulting spaces. Also make a space to record his efforts and improvements over previous periods. Give him a gold star for excellent work, silver for good, and red or blue for other performances. Especially if he is the only student, your child needs some visible and tangible evidence of his progress in every area. In competing with his own past accomplishments, he has an incentive to do even better.

Record Progress

We also recommend that you fill out weekly assignment sheets for each of your students and place them into a folder. This will help your students to see what is expected of them during the week in every subject, even in the area of homework assignments. This can also provide you with a sense of direction and accomplishment in your weekly schedule.

Read Aloud

Have students at all grade levels read aloud several times a week. You might have them read aloud into a tape recorder, then listen to themselves while following along in the book and noting errors. This activity can help improve reading skills and articulation.

Read aloud to your K–6 students each day if possible. Many studies reveal that reading aloud to children can help them develop their own reading skills. In one study, instructors read aloud to 20 classes of seven year olds for 20 minutes a day for one school year.

At the end of that time, the children were tested and compared with another group to whom the teacher had not read aloud. The read-aloud group showed significantly higher gains in vocabulary and reading comprehension. Make sure the readings are stimulating and exciting enough to hold their interest while you are building their imaginations. Keep the initial readings short enough to fit their attention spans and gradually lengthen both. Let your child associate reading with pleasure. Reward him by reading aloud to him, rather than by giving him candy.

Stay the Course

Do not become discouraged if this is your first year homeschooling. Parents all over the nation have confirmed that homeschool responsibilities become more manageable with time. Remember, you are investing for the future, and your time and effort will result in rich family dividends that cannot be measured in dollars and cents. "Be strong and of good courage; do not be afraid, nor be dismayed, for the LORD your God is with you wherever you go" (Joshua 1:9).

Teaching Several Children

by Meg Johnson[11]

Teaching children of different ages naturally takes a great deal of planning and time. Parents become very concerned about school lessons, but children need time with their parents for more than schooling. They also deserve personal care and attention, opportunities to help Mom and Dad with projects, and so on. Meeting all these needs can be quite a challenge. This article offers suggestions for organizing your school program to teach children at different levels without neglecting your preschoolers or other home responsibilities. Because we are deeply concerned about our responsibilities for educating our children, trying to meet all the needs at once creates most of the strain. We teach our children more than academics. Let us examine other areas of guiding and nurturing them.

Meeting Individual Needs

Children are all different. Even siblings may differ greatly in readiness and learning styles. Be flexible. A program or learning environment which meets the needs of one child may simply not fit the next child's abilities, interests, or aptitudes.

Because homeschooling families enjoy close relationships, parents can easily capitalize on their children's individual readiness—and more importantly, they can adjust to accommodate

---

11. Meg Johnson, "Teaching Several Children," in *The Home School Manual*, ed. Theodore E. Wade, Jr. (Auburn, CA: Gazelle Publications, 1988), pp. 320–326.

each child's differences in readiness among various learning areas. Take time to find out what your children can, should, or want to be learning at each age or grade level. Parents should then provide materials and an environment to help each child learn as he is ready.

Now let us look at a few ideas which might help in organizing activities so that you can be available to teach your older children and still have time to spend with the younger ones. Start by planning space for your school room. You need a routine place to work and to localize the mess that results occasionally from art projects, crafts, or science experiments.

Using Space Efficiently

You need to be able to change easily from working with one child to working with another. Positioning desks or tables so that you can move around and sit between children often works well. You need to be able to work with one child while being right there to answer the questions of the others. Encourage children not directly involved with you during this time to do something that interests them or give them something to do that will occupy them so they are not disruptive. Make a place for toddlers and young children to play adjacent to or in the working area. This may cause a certain amount of disruption, but if each person realizes that he must work and pay attention, lessons can continue and progress will occur. When a quieter atmosphere is needed for concentration, individual children can go to another room temporarily. This arrangement may not be ideal, but most of the time it works better than you might expect.

Teamwork

Younger children pick up quite a bit of basic knowledge and skills from being exposed to the learning environment of older siblings and by imitating their behavior. Far less explaining may be needed for these younger children when it comes time to learn some of the concepts already taught to their big brothers and sisters. But remember that while getting ideas across to the younger children may be faster, each child deserves quality time  with his parents—investigating the world and working and doing things with them. Bonds of love and understanding formed between parent and child during early years generally hold when adolescent counseling is needed and, in fact, throughout life.

Older children, especially if they have always been homeschooled, should have developed good independent study habits. Setting a goal of getting work done without being prodded can teach responsibility. Make reasonable assignments, and require that each day's work be done even if it means continuing after your regular school time. When a child has reached a point of independence in his own work, he can be relied on as needed to take care of very young siblings—changing diapers, keeping an eye on them, and so on. He can also learn to assist younger siblings with their learning by answering questions, explaining directions, or teaching concepts he himself has mastered. This helping can be part of the child's own school program. From the very beginning, each child should understand that he is responsible for getting his work done, and that siblings and the home teacher are there mainly to assist. Also, teach your children to always give others consideration when interrupting or asking for assistance.

Being a "teacher's assistant" to younger children can be a valuable learning experience for older siblings. It reinforces their own learning and develops more of an awareness of others' needs. Younger children pick up concepts and facts by listening to discussions of older siblings, and older children understand better by teaching the younger. Because of this crossover learning, a great deal of reinforcement occurs. This strength of family cooperation and an environment that is usually calm lead to good learning and thinking skills.

Using Time Efficiently

Challenges do arise, however, when you will wish you were several people at once. For instance, older children might need to have new concepts explained or to do research or experiments which require adult assistance; infants or toddlers may need to be watched and cared for; and a six or seven year old may want to learn about some unit which requires an adult to read or help him get started. Each child needs time and attention. In such situations, just evaluate as quickly as possible how to most effectively distribute time and attention. Usually in a few moments older children can be guided in the right direction to work until you can get back to them; someone can meet the youngest child's need; and with little delay, time can be devoted to your less mature scholar. Under your organized management, your children will learn to do what they can on their own, so you can meet the needs of whoever cannot go ahead alone.

To help make your teaching easier and efficient, plan as many units as feasible which involve all your students. A general topic like airplanes can have many teaching activities. Certain ones, of course, will be too easy or too hard for some of your children. If you remember the varying abilities of your listeners and hold different expectations, they will understand, and your teaching will be surprisingly successful. You may want to write your study questions in order of increasing difficulty, assigning work for a specific student up to a certain item number. In other instances you can plan team projects with roles assigned (or permitted to be chosen) according to ability.

Of course, it is not always possible or easy to have all of your students learning about the same subject at the same time, if they differ in age and work at different levels. Occasionally—although not as frequently as we would like—the younger children will learn from and be interested in the activities of the older ones. Most of the time, however, your children will need to do completely different activities. Experience and trial-and-error will help you plan wisely and see when to change your plan. If all this sounds like it could easily lead to chaos, try it. Usually you will find that, despite some confusion, activities can continue and good progress will be made.

Good planning can limit the amount of your time each child will need. On the average, a child may need one to two hours a day. Your contact time may overlap considerably if two children work together, or if you can supervise more than one at different activities. However, when homeschooling involves more than one child, the entire morning or occasionally even more time may have to be devoted to directing learning activities and to meeting the school needs of your children. On many days the time you spend solely in teaching may be much less than this, but plan to commit a good portion of each day to your children. You must be available when needed and must provide guidance and supervision.

Parents do not actually have to spend as much time formally teaching their children as you might expect. Many subjects, such as science, history, geography, social sciences, and [Bible or theological studies] need discussion, practical application, experimentation, and outside trips. Try to provide opportunities and materials so your children can explore these areas. Take time to investigate with your children. While this demands time and energy, and housework does not always get done, it really can be a lot of fun. Of course, books are valuable

HOW A TREE GROWS

tools too, if used carefully. They provide an efficient way of sharing accumulated knowledge and facts. At home, a good balance can easily be achieved between book learning and application.

Some specific ways to teach effectively include simple ideas such as a daily routine (which should be flexible, but fairly consistent), yearly and daily goals, written guidelines for the children to follow so they know what it is they should be doing, and a place to work which is as conducive to "school work" as possible. Also, in order to give older children time to be helped, their learning should be designed to fit their needs. Limit unnecessary repetition of concepts and skills they have already mastered. Use materials with clear instructions and explanations of concepts.

Building Character

Help your children develop a sense of personal responsibility for their school work and for helping around the house.

The home-school learning environment lacks the classroom atmosphere with pressure from peers and teachers to enforce performance and discipline. Therefore, the various demands and activities of the home environment give children a more immediate need to develop self-discipline, self-motivation, and initiative. Because these character traits are not easy to form, parents must help their children realize the need for them in their work and study tasks.

As much as possible, let the needs for responsible behavior lead to its natural development. Children may take advantage of disorder or a brother's or sister's demand for attention to fool around or disrupt the schooling. It may then be wise to discuss what each child should contribute to a more pleasant environment for everyone. Such correcting experiences help build character. As a child realizes that out of consideration for the needs of his siblings and parents, he should be responsible for tending to business, he becomes more motivated to work on his own. Self-direction takes time to develop, however, so be willing to oversee your child's work. Check regularly to see that he understands and completes his tasks.

As a teacher, be with your children during their learning activities, even if you must sit between two of them guiding their schoolwork with a younger child on each knee! Each of your children deserves time and loving attention. Even though you are only one person, if you are close by, you can give each child as much attention as possible.

Although your home school may be less than perfect, remember that its consistent environment, the demands it makes on each family member, and your children's achievement of self-discipline from contributing to everyone's welfare make it the best place for developing good habits of learning and helping. Leading your children to good behavior is an essential part of their education. Just as children who attend classroom schools may get up in the morning and say they do not want to go, homeschooled children may refuse to do their school work cheerfully or to cooperate with chores. You can discuss with them the importance of cooperation and consideration for others. The intimacy of the home dramatically emphasizes the effects of each person's actions. Although a day of school lessons may occasionally seem to be "lost" to character building efforts, over the long term a definite maturity will evolve in the children's attitudes about working independently and assisting each other. They will gradually be able to work on their own and become valuable contributors to the household operation.

As you watch this development, your children's contributions to the family's life will balance the burdens of parenting and of home schooling. You may spend a lot of time and effort, but you will be pleased with and thankful for the results. It is a most rewarding challenge!

Getting Everything Done

by Meg Johnson[12]

One of the most frightening aspects of homeschooling is the question of how to get everything done. The days never seem long enough even without home school. Then when the teaching responsibility is added on top of it all, how can a person adequately meet all the family's needs? The ideal is no doubt impossible, but with careful planning we can do much more than we think.

Meeting Personal Needs

Home schoolers have generally decided that personal needs of each family member are top priority. These include communication, physical care, opportunities to enjoy individual interests, and educational guidance, to name just a few. As we discuss personal needs let us consider three categories. Most demanding are the *needs of the children*. Second come the *needs of the spouse*. And last, there are the *needs of the person responsible for the home teaching*, usually the mother. The whole family should contribute to satisfying these needs, but often the major burden falls on the mother and teacher. One person cannot do it all, however, so the entire family must be committed to the goals of home education. Individuals occasionally will need to forego personal gratifications.

Needs of the Children

Adequately caring for each child's needs can be quite a challenge, especially if two or more are under eight years of age. But even if the mother must divide her attention among several children and her other responsibilities, she still gives each child much more

---

12. Meg Johnson, "Getting Everything Done," in *The Home School Manual*, ed. Theodore E. Wade, Jr. (Auburn, CA: Gazelle Publications, 1988), pp. 330–335.

time and individual loving attention than could ever be received in a classroom school. Also, sharing and taking turns and waiting for attention are best learned in a family. Such goals require effort from both children and parents, but proper social behavior learned at home will be valuable to your children when they are on their own.

Planning does not dictate every move. Actual decisions about who needs attention minute by minute are usually obvious. The baby needs a diaper change; a young learner can not go on until a concept is explained; the telephone rings (some home schoolers ignore this); and so on. Three to six year-olds are probably the most easily neglected when there are several children in the family. They tend to need less guidance in learning than older children and require less physical care than the younger ones. They will often go and play quietly when you ask them to, but they still need and deserve your undivided attention for a part of each day.

Have you ever felt at the end of a long day that all you have done is run from one need to another with no time for your own interests? Remember that those who have children around all day often feel this way. Just balance these frustrating times against the days when you do see significant progress. Even though your accomplishments may not be obvious like shiny quarts of apple sauce lined up on the shelf, you have had the opportunity to provide an atmosphere of love for each family member. As you work with each child, you can plant seeds for positive character building in a way that could not possibly be matched in a classroom. Even if you do not see much change day by day, when you look over several months or a year, you should see significant accomplishments spiritually and emotionally as well as intellectually. Your children's real needs will be met.

Needs of the Spouse

Here you face another great challenge. As both mother and teacher, your children's needs often demand your first attention; but never satisfy them at the expense of your marriage relationship. You might not have as much time as you would like to be with your husband during this period in your family's development. But allot special time for communicating. Discuss responsibilities and roles. The husband is the focal point of your family's activity and the foundation on which your home school rests. Usually he must make significant sacrifices to provide a home environment so the mother can devote large portions of time to her children instead of to him, to home-making, or to helping earn the family income.

Mother is usually the teacher, but the roles may be reversed or not so clearly differentiated. While the father may spend little time in actual teaching, his contribution is of paramount importance to ultimate success. His participation in raising his children enhances their learning and enjoyment. His patience while the mother must devote a great deal of her energy to homeschooling, considerably lessens her burden of having to meet everyone's needs while all too often no one seems to be interested in meeting hers. The father also provides a model for his children to emulate. In discussing home schools, much is often said about cooperation between parents, because all too often, if they are not united, it does not work at all.

Dad, as I see it, the environment you help provide adds a dimension to your life. Both you and your children can certainly be enriched. Even though you may feel you are giving up personal time, you reap great rewards. When out with your children, you will have many reasons to be very pleased with them. Home-schooled children tend to be calmer, more considerate, more independent, and more thoughtful than many children who spend large periods of time with their peers.

Needs of the Home Teacher

Mom, you are not likely to find much time for personal interests and relaxation until the children are old enough to help take care of themselves. But do set aside some time to relax. Ask the rest of the family to help out. And just remember that this heavy schedule is temporary. The rewards will more than compensate.

Planning and Teaching

In addition to responsibilities for the personal needs of each family member, planning your school program and teaching demand large blocks of time. We never have all the time we would like to do things with our children. Even letting them explore and learn on their own takes a lot of time. Take a good look at what you do, not on a daily basis, but over the long term. Set goals, of course, but avoid getting despondent when the days just are not long enough.

Using Programs Wisely

If you use structured home study courses, you may sometimes feel overwhelmed by what is expected. Remember that because you work closely with your children and have a sense of the learning appropriate for their level, you are the best judge of what they know and need to study. Whenever possible, select a structured program that is flexible enough to permit your student to work at his or her own pace. If you enroll your child in a course, make every effort to help him or her learn the course material. Just be sensitive to individual needs and abilities. Use tests to

make sure your child is grasping the course material. Many home study courses are based on programs used in schools with children of differing abilities, and they often provide more material than may be needed for a particular individual. Try to utilize structured programs that pre-test their students in order to determine a course of study that is individually tailored to your child.

Good programs offer a selection of ideas and materials so that the home schooler may draw on the knowledge, experience, and efforts of many people. Let your home study courses enhance your teaching rather than create pressures which might interfere with it.

Training Children to Help

For a time-efficient home school, encourage your children to develop independent study habits. Older children to a large degree must learn to teach themselves and to assist each other, as well as younger children.

Children can develop the skills and initiative to contribute a great deal to the life of their family. They can care for younger siblings, help in the kitchen or with other household chores, and work in the yard or garden. Gradually, your children's attitudes about work will change from seeing chores as tedious to feeling that they are helping you and contributing to the family needs.

Teaching your children how to work thoroughly and cheerfully is worth the time and patience. Although maturing children cannot do things as well or quickly as you can, accept their efforts in contributing to the comfort of the home, and your life together will be rewarding.

Establishing a Viable Routine

In our family, the days are divided informally into time blocks. Mornings belong to book learning, and Mom is available for teaching and assistance during these hours. For us, "schoolwork" must be done first. Afternoons are devoted to other activities which may include baking, household chores, sewing, home maintenance, community service, individual projects, or visits with other home schoolers. Although we have found home schooling to be a full-time demanding lifestyle, it becomes easier as the children grow up. As they mature they become aware of what needs to be done and can help around the home on their own.

In addition to having flexible daily time blocks, we generally follow the regular public school vacation schedule. While home schooling really involves constant learning and growing, our normal program is limited to the school schedule of the children's peers. Vacations and weekends offer good breaks to relax and catch up on unfinished chores and projects. We all enjoy our vacations, but we also find it a relief to return to our regular routine, even though it is quite flexible.

In addition to routine and unavoidable chores, it may sometimes help to accomplish or work on one special project a day. On some days you may simply want to make learning more meaningful. On other days you could take time out to do a family or household project, go somewhere special, do extra shopping, make a doctor visit, or just get ahead in schoolwork. Each family defines, however flexibly, its own patterns and goals as home schooling is integrated into the family lifestyle.

Developing Accountability

Specific planning and record keeping makes working independently easier for the children. At the beginning of each day, we usually make an outline of what is to be done. The students can then go on and do their work even if no one is there to watch them every minute. And I can tend to other household and child-care demands, as necessary, during school hours. Of course, children cannot always be left unsupervised as they may dawdle and bicker, but they become more responsible as time goes on. Eventually they realize that they must do their work. When older children work on their own, you have time to meet some of the needs of the younger ones. Also, in addition to writing out what is planned for the day, we keep a record of what has been accomplished.

Looking at the Big Picture

Although homeschooling family lifestyles tend to revolve around the children, there is more to be done than teaching. Housework and meal preparation demand attention, too. Well-organized home-school families function efficiently but still face limitations of time and energy. In many families the first thing to slip is the housework. Until the older children can responsibly help with this, it is difficult for the mother to manage all her responsibilities. Some may have children around all day and still keep the house spotless. They are exceptions.

Our family finally had to set a few basic goals. We try to clean up before Daddy gets home to make a little room for him in our small house. We do try to keep our living room fairly neat—a challenge with a toddler. Major cleaning is done when possible but never on the weekly basis that once seemed so necessary. We seriously try to keep up on only the dishes and laundry, and we make time to plan and prepare good meals. Someday we may have everything under control, but for now, housekeeping is a low priority.

In our frenzied struggle to do everything we think we should, let us remember that our lives have purpose. Days devoted to raising children who will have firm character and moral values are days well-spent.

Using Textbooks Effectively

by Marvin Eicher

There was a time when the Bible and a dictionary were the two main textbooks available to many teachers. Today that has all been changed. Now there are textbooks for teaching everything from arithmetic to geography; from art to typing. The question for teachers is no longer so much what to teach as how to teach it effectively. Following are a few pointers on how to derive the greatest benefit from the textbooks used in the classroom.

Be Well Acquainted with the Material

A textbook is a learning tool, and we cannot expect to use any tool effectively if we are not familiar with it. Imagine an auto mechanic who purchases a new tool but then neglects to learn about its functions and uses. He will be seriously limited in his ability to use that tool in repairing automobiles. In the same way, the effectiveness of a teacher is seriously limited if he is not acquainted with his material.

Become familiar with the basic philosophy underlying the textbooks you use. Know the author's primary objectives and the means by which he intends that they be achieved. As much as possible, make his goals your goals—this should not be difficult if the textbook is written from a Christian perspective. If it is not, you do well to be informed about objectives you cannot support so that you can do what is possible to counter them.

Know the overall content and layout of the textbook. Get an idea of the general progression of thought from beginning to end. Find out how often there are reviews and tests. All these things are essential to a thorough acquaintance with the textbook so that you can use it in the most effective way possible.

Develop a Plan for Your Particular Class

Determine how much material should be covered each day, each week, and each month, and devise a schedule with check points along the way to measure your progress. Be sure to allow time for reviews and tests. You need not feel strictly bound to your plan, but at least it will provide a gauge that will show whether or not you will get through the book.

You will also want to allow room for adjustments along the way if the need arises. Which parts of the book are basic and must be emphasized? Which parts are less important? Familiarity with the textbook is essential to the answering of these questions.

Avoid Being a Slave to the Textbook

Always remember that *you* are the teacher, and you know your particular class. Therefore, set out to teach your pupils what you know they need. If a certain course has a teacher's guide, do not feel obligated to carry out every suggestion it contains. Rather, use the teacher's guide as a means of accomplishing

your goals in the most effective way for your particular students. Textbooks are an important aid in teaching the various subjects; but in the end you will be the one who determines how effectively the material is conveyed.[13]

---

13. Students enrolled in CLASS Administration Plan need to follow the course instructions, which give specific details for properly completing any given course.

Teaching Art and Music at Home

If you are looking for new ways to enrich your home education program and to make learning for your students fresh and exciting, you may want to consider the integration of art and music with other subjects in your curriculum. Integration with other courses, if structured properly, will help meet the requirements for art and music in the homeschooling setting.

There is an old saying, "The art of the times is the expression of the times." This means that the visual arts—painting and sculpture—and the music of a particular historical period express the values and aspirations of the people of that time. To know something of the art and music of a people is to gain a certain understanding of the time in which they lived. Such an approach to learning can make the dry study of facts and events more exciting and rewarding for both student and teacher. For example, in history, by exposing a student to the art and music of a particular period, the culture of that period begins to take shape in his mind. As a result, his study of history will have greater depth and meaning.

At first thought, this process might seem difficult or complicated. Actually, it is quite simple. If you make a visit to your local library, you will be surprised at the variety and amount of resource material available on this topic.

In the area of music, there is an excellent series called *History Alive through Music* available from Holly Hall Publications.[14] The series consists of three books, each accompanied by a professionally recorded audiocassette. Each book or cassette presents a different perspective on music in American history through stories, photographs, sheet music, chord charts, and recorded music.

---

14. Holly Hall Publications can be ordered through Appalachian Distributors, 522 Princeton Road, Johnson City, TN 37601 or by phone at (423) 282-9475.

For those who wish to enrich their study of geography, there is a great deal of music from the various nations catalogued under folk music of the world.

In short, there is a wealth of audio/visual materials available at your local library. If certain materials are not available locally, your librarian may be able to order them. If you have not already done so, get acquainted with your local library. By integrating art and music into your curriculum, you can add a new dimension to your program.

You will not find them at your local library, but there are a couple of fine resources available from Cornerstone Curriculum.[15] Cornerstone is operated by David and Shirley Quine, who home school their nine children. *Adventures in Art*, based on the works of Dr. Francis Schaeffer, illustrates the interaction between art and philosophy in Western civilization. *Music & Moments with the Masters* will open up the world of classical music and demonstrate the impact of ideas on culture.

---

15. You may contact Cornerstone Curriculum at (972) 235–5149, or visit them online at <www.cornerstonecurriculum.com>.

Never Lose Faith in Your Child

by Dr. Paul A. Kienel

When our Lord selected His twelve disciples, He did not choose candidates whose academic records showed them to be in the top ten percent of their class. He used the meekest of men, most of whom were totally uneducated to perpetuate His gospel to all future generations.

Even at less lofty levels than the Lord's disciples, there have been men who were honored in their adult years as great leaders, but as children in school they were perpetual candidates for the "least likely to succeed" group.

Perhaps a classic example is the well-known story of a boy named Albert. Albert was so slow to learn to talk that his parents thought he was abnormal. His teachers called him a misfit and his classmates avoided him. He failed his first college entrance examination. To the amazement of everyone, he turned out to be one of the greatest scientists in the world. His name was Albert Einstein.

Winston Churchill was less than a bright boy in school. As a matter of fact, he was the lowest achiever in his class all the way through his early years of education. He stuttered so badly that his parents and teachers could barely understand him. In later years, as Prime Minister of Great Britain, he became known as one of the most eloquent statesmen in history. In 1953, he won the Nobel Prize for Literature.

Winston Churchill (1874–1965)

If your youngster is struggling in school, do not lose faith in him. There is hope! Of course, success in later life is not guaranteed to the youngster who struggles in school even as success is not assured the student who is a "straight 'A' genius." It is interesting to observe how many times children who trudge a continual uphill road in school develop a quality of determination in their character that makes them valuable citizens in their later years. If your youngster is less than an "academic whiz," perhaps you will take comfort in the following survey of 342 graduates of Columbia University. According to the findings, "Those who had graduated from Columbia University with honors, who had won scholastic medals, who had been elected to Phi Beta Kappa, were more likely to be in the lower professional levels than in the top levels!"

I suppose the best interpretation of such findings is that students who always succeed in school never learn the valuable lessons reserved only for strugglers and uphill climbers. Those who whiz through school very often have some basic qualities of determination missing from their fibers and are afraid to attempt anything where the risk of failure is a possibility. This is not to say that you have to be mentally dull and have a difficult time in school to succeed in life. Brilliance is not a liability. But in the Lord's economy of people, He has graciously balanced the scales and our worth to the kingdom is not determined totally on our academic prowess. God can use dim bulbs as well as bright bulbs! He can take our liabilities and turn them into assets and our lives will bring honor to His name so long as we are willing to submit ourselves to His direction.

Our number one responsibility as parents is to guide our children to a total commitment to Jesus Christ and to trust Him completely for life's direction (Proverbs 3:5–6).

> *Trust in the Lord with all your heart; and lean not to your own understanding. In all your ways acknowledge Him, and He shall direct your paths.*
>
> *Proverbs 3:5–6*

Whatever the natural liabilities and handicaps your child may have in school, his potential worth to the world is greatly enhanced if he loves God and has strong love ties at home. Your child can weather every storm if he knows that Christ loves him and his parents love him. It is imperative to the mental and emotional well-being of your child that love be expressed to him by his parents on a regular basis and in a variety of ways. I am sure observers of our household would characterize us as an affectionate family. My wife and I kiss our three daughters at least once each day and express words of parental affection to them. My wife and I also kiss each other in full view of our children. In addition to the fact that the common cold spreads rapidly in our household, there is a lot of genuine family love in our home. In my view, next to our love for Christ should be our constant love for our families. The family is the basic unit of society and its cohesiveness is based on love.

Your child's ability to surmount the everyday pressures of school, church, and neighborhood are enhanced many times over if he has the security of God's love in his heart, and the security of knowing that he has a home where he is understood and loved. As valuable as Christian school education is, it is secondary to a Christian home where Christ-honoring love flows freely. The church and the Christian school are service institutions serving families and helping parents to train up their children "… in the way they should go."

Never lose faith in your child. There is hope for him. There is hope especially if the love of Christ is pre-eminent in your child's home, church, and school.